'Just as I am' is dedicated to my amazing Mam and Dad, my brother Peter, my wonderful second mum, Lesley, and my best friend Nicky. Thank for your unending support and loving me as 'me'.

Note from the author

How do I control niggling worries and thoughts? I used to be such a worrier about the smallest things that made me feel uncomfortable – like speaking out and making myself known. I would much prefer it if no one knew I was there. When I woke up in Intensive Care, I was reliant on other people for everything – I couldn't even speak to tell them what I needed. *That* was uncomfortable. Over time I had to almost teach my body how to do everything again in order to regain my independence. I learnt an awful lot from that bad experience. I would much rather tolerate something that is uncomfortable for maybe an hour or two (or less), if it might prevent someone else experiencing some of the uncomfortable things I have. That is the long and short of it. I can't change my past, and I wouldn't want to. The bad is just as much a part of me and without it, I wouldn't have the good things. What I can do is try to change things for others and make their lives better.

How did I become so contented? I think it was when I accepted who I am – what I am. I have no wish to be anyone other than myself. I love me as me. Be yourself. If others choose not to like who you are, it is their loss – not yours.

When did it happen? I suppose the hospital was the 'moment' – the intensive care unit was where the acceptance started, although I probably didn't know it then. I woke up and I was stripped bare (not literally – I did have a hospital gown!)

It was like the slate was wiped clean of all the rubbish – the bullying and depression and all the bad bits washed away with my illness. I think more of the good memories now, when I think of

Ally Schofield

First Published in 2025 by LV Publishing

Print ISBN: 978-1-7391381-9-6

my past – and there was a lot of good. It was all overshadowed before, but now I can begin again. I came home from hospital with a refreshed outlook on life, happy to accept my limitations, so I can enjoy what I can do and the things I know I'm capable of. I stopped trying to be something I am not.

I don't pretend to be 'all-knowing' – none of us humans are, but there is something in being at death's door and realising what you are about to leave behind. It gave me the courage not to give up. All I want now is for my loved ones to be happy and healthy and to be able to help as many people as I can. Despite all we hear in the news, I believe there is a lot of good in the world and that is worth holding onto – especially through difficult times.

Thank you to all my family and friends who gave me permission to put in poems I wrote in memory of loved ones; I can't tell you how much it means to me to be able to include them in my collection.

Thank you Mam and Dad, and other members of my amazing family, for being my muses when I can't find the word I'm looking for!

A huge thank you also to my Mam, and friends, Barbara Maddocks, Fielda and David Kemp, Mary and Norman Craik, and John Langley for helping me with proof-reading and other advice and encouragement, which enabled me to put my collection together.

You might notice that within some of the poems there are capitals or lower case where you wouldn't expect them to be. It was pointed out to me in proof-reading. I have chosen to leave them like that because I feel it demonstrates the different way in which my mind works – it is how I think when I write.

I am happier and more contented than I have ever been. I saw the end and it reminded me why I am here. I know what my purpose is. If sharing my experiences helps just one other person, then it makes all the bad bits worth it and my purpose has been fulfilled. If you are reading my book, thank you and if I can offer some advice to you, it is this:

Everyone is different. Amongst all the self-help books in the world, not one will suit every person who 'falls' into its category. We are individuals and should be treated and valued as such. Let us all help each other. Each one of us can only do our best in the circumstances we find ourselves in.

No one can be a better you. Remember that.

Ally

Contents

A Window into Critical Illness 61

Where My Heart Is 131

Behind the locker door

I would like to dedicate the section 'Behind the locker door' to everyone who has accepted me as being 'me' and those who have helped me to get where I am today.

Miss Kate Evans (my childhood ENT consultant in Gloucestershire) and Chris Till, who looked after me so well in Audiology as a child, are two of many who 'started the ball rolling'!

Thank you also to Mr Kempshall for sorting out my dislocating knees!

To my friends, Nicky, Clair and Imogen, thank you for standing by me throughout primary school and helping to 'weather' the bullying and my friend Charlotte, thank you for always being there for me at secondary school and ever since.

To my brilliant boarding school, Mary Hare, especially all the teachers and Care staff, and my friends, thank you for your guidance through such a difficult time in my life. Sophie, Kirsty, Mikhail, Hamish, Clare, Georgia and Faye, to name some of many. 'Not through rose-tinted glasses' is dedicated to you all.

Thank you to everyone at Brampton poets for your kindness and support – I am so grateful to be part of the group.

'Dressed in black' is especially for my family and friends.

A special mention to the fantastic physio team at Carleton Clinic who are doing such a fabulous job working with me to improve my life. You are all amazing – thank you.

The poems 'Ataxia', 'The words I speak' and 'The power of Haggis and physiotherapists' are for you.

'A short guide to understanding 'ME" and 'The life of a diabetic' are dedicated to the genetics team and the diabetes team up north - thank you for finding out 'who' I am! The latter is also dedicated to Dr Akroyd, my childhood diabetes consultant, who Mam once had to ring when I was ill in India – sorry for interrupting your holiday but thank you for your help!

The colleagues I worked with in such a lovely little primary school (especially the staff who braved the weather with me – and are still braving it today!) – thank you for giving me a chance and I really loved working with you and the children. The poem about being a lunchtime supervisor is dedicated to you and all the children I looked after.

The sweetness of my life

At one point if you'd asked me,
I'd have said it was the worst;
That being a diabetic,
Would make my bubble burst,
But then one day I learnt something,
That saved me from despair,
When I realized I was not alone,
It wasn't so hard to bear.

Chocolate this and chocolate that,
It was my favourite thing,
Ice cream and jelly babies,
Would be sure to make me sing,
Give me a doughnut any day,
Filled with jam and cream,
But now I know there's more to life,
Than sweet food and ice cream.

Fairy cakes, gingerbread men,
Whether morning or afternoon;
I liked making banana cake -
Especially licking the spoon!
I loved all seasonal chocolate,
Especially egg-shaped and sweet;
Apple pie and hot custard
Would sweep me off my feet.

Just As I Am

Tasty Raspberry cheesecake
Would definitely make me beam,
Strawberries, and for goodness sake;
Don't forget the cream.
Profiteroles with chocolate sauce
Were mouth-watering in my book,
A chilling ice cream sundae
Got an Oliver-look.

Jelly and Blancmange,
Was something I enjoyed,
A luscious chocolate cake,
Would make me jump for joy;
Give me a scone any day,
Filled with jam and cream,
But my life is sweet enough
Without sugar-coated dreams.

Ally Schofield

A short guide to understanding 'ME'

Ataxia – struggles with balance and gait
Is just the first thing on my plate.
Diabetes since my 13th year;
Peaks and Plummeting do occur.
Deafness since six years old,
Raynaud's phenomenon – I feel the cold.
Hypermobility; bends and twists;
Broken toes and sprained wrists.
Mallet deformity, a weakening grip,
Another stumble or a slip.
Bendy toes, a folding foot;
Neuro-physio has an input.
Hips are sore, knees give way;
In that I don't get a say.
Irlen's syndrome, sometime a tremor;
It's quite a list to remember!
Oh I forgot – the memory's lacking;
Causes my nerves a bit of flapping.
So who am I? Do you feel educated?
Well I am 'ME'– as I stated.

Look through our eyes

We see a different world –
Yours is straight – ours is curled
Among bungalows just one skyscraper
Or think of a lonely sheet of paper,
A blank page, white as snow,
Unknown land where new things grow.

Your view of things to us is unclear
On the paper, only outlines appear
– they are thick like charcoal,
We quite easily fall down a hole
It gives us chaos, adding shade
And we're unnerved when clarity fades.
Layers will give us more confusion
Which ends up with our exclusion.

We are many – but all to often
Others treat us with worried caution;
We get left in shadows on our own
to be different – is to be alone.

It does not make us any less
Our feelings we can still express;
We find beauty that others don't –
And see the things that they won't
the hidden jewels reach our eyes,
It can be a blessing in disguise.

But really we are the same as you;
we just have a different view.
Just as people have different opinions
And a person has their own dominion;
So please don't run
And before you shun,

Before you make our beating hearts sink;
Hold your horses – Stop and think.
Consider what it is you imply
And try to look through our eyes.

Bird song for my broken ears

I heard the birds up in the sky,
It made me stop and give a sigh.
A sound that means to me so much;
In the harshest moment; a gentle touch.
They sing through wind and pouring rain;
Their song can soothe the deepest pain.
These sounds I hear; I really treasure;
And the memory of them I hold forever.

Bird song for my broken ears

Ally Schofield

Little corner shy

Imagine a little girl, with pigtails,
Stood in a corner alone,
Crying out for a candle,
To break through the darkness,
But the darkness is made of stone.

She is deaf to the world,
So the world is deaf to her,
In silence, she comforts herself,
Bullies? The teachers say report them,
Do the teachers seem bothered? No sir.

Day after day, more terrified she grows,
Floundering as if she were on fire,
Plunging down beneath the underworld,
Help me please, her cries grow still louder,
Only to be branded a worthless whiner.

This little girl, so desperate she was,
But they only ever saw her as a curse,
It's bad enough, guttering in water,
Horrific even, choking on poison,
But drowning in nothing is worse.

The lucky ones escape this nightmare,
The lucky ones hold the key,
But there are some who, still are trapped,
Forgive me please for the lecture,
But that little girl used to be me.

Ataxia

Sometimes I need a hand -
I fall like a wall of sand.
There's not always a mechanical reason,
For my body will commit a treason,
Let me down at my own cost
And my balance is all but lost.

Often I can coo or croon
But my brain sings to the wrong tune.
The feeling I get is wearing thin;
At times I wonder if I feel the earth spin.
It shakes me right through my core,
For I find myself on the floor.

Also not helpful is the dark;
It's like the hunting of the snark.
Where do things start; where do they end?
On my pins I can't depend.
And like the reason for many a war,
I don't know what I'm looking for.
When the horizon disappears from sight,
Every step becomes a fight,
But even in day it's hard to cope;
Paths can seem as narrow as rope.

Hypermobility is also tricky;
Situations become a bit sticky.
Often I can learn the lines,
But I still can't read the signs
My joints just don't comply,
Sun eclipsed by cloudy sky.

My joints make a sudden change
And all the words are re-arranged.

Disagreeable too is uneven ground;
Gravel and cobbles see me downed.
My ankles wobble and then collapse,
Melting ice cream and jelly perhaps.

With such events I'm learning to cope
And that gives me a lot of hope.
With help I am finding solid ground,
Matching steps with the right sound.
With the right aid I can work to re-train
And re-wire my unusual brain.

Ataxia

Don't look at us like cake

When they looked at me;
it wasn't me they saw.
They saw a cake half eaten;
but I am so much more.

When people hear 'disabilities'
no matter what they are;
some immediately assume
'that person won't get far'

They decide they know
if we are capable or not.
But believe me;
- that is utter rot.

We are individuals,
With different strengths to yours.
And we are just as deserving
of newly-opened doors.

So to be a better person,
kind and not opaque,
Think twice before assuming,
and don't look at us like cake.

Our qualities shout out loudly,
And we see things another way.
Oh, we can really shine,
If you listen to what we say.

So instead of fearing disabilities,
Value the gifts we bring.
Celebrate our differences,
And give us a song to sing.

Imagination

Gathering swallows twitter
In a beautiful glade,
And through cascading water,
Lumbering hippos wade.

I dream that I can hear,
A cricket orchestra sing.
The gift of imagination
Is a wonderful thing.

It gives a glimmer of hope,
In a burnt orange glow.
I lap up the atmosphere,
As thoughts grow and grow.

In a kaleidoscope of colours,
The world is warmly bathed.
And for a brand new dawn,
A welcome path is paved.

Not a thundering avalanche,
Nor a perilous sea.
A never-thriving meadow,
Nor a dried-up stream.

Nothing can destroy this moment,
Or take these things I've seen.
My mind is my own,
For in my head I've been.

Beautiful chaos

Parrots squawking;
A jaguar stalking;
Rabbits playing;
Trees are swaying.

A pretty striking
purple rose;
expect thorns
as the saying goes,

Penguins waddle;
Seagulls squabble;
Monkeys chatter;
Elephants swagger;

Frogs are leaping;
Darkness creeping;
Lions roaring;
Streams are pouring.

Geese are calling;
Raindrops falling;
To the flora's pleasure,
The heavy-grey's treasure.

Tigers slinking
Without blinking;
A flat-footed panda
Has a good gander.

Just As I Am

Crocodiles snapping;
Rhinos crashing;
Hippos bellow;
Daffodil yellow.

The light is dimpled;
Stars will twinkle;
Rivers rushing;
A pear is blushing.

Peacock struts;
Flytrap shuts;
Water cascades
In the glade.

Sandy beaches;
Donut peaches;
Sun rays glimmer;
Concrete shimmers.

There's a banana that
 is strangely red;
An urchin living
on the sea bed;

An emperor tulip
With a pointy tip;
The seasons fleeting;
Little lambs bleating;
The moon will glisten;
Meerkats listen.

Owls hooting
in the night;

The clouds are bathing
in silver light.

Majestic snapdragon
an army of spires;
The uplifting singing
of a choir.

A mountain towering
high above;
flying up,
a small white dove.

The soothing sound
of nature's music;
So many gorgeous
things to pick.

Leaves are floating,
do you want more?
A mosiac on
the forest floor.

A Polar bear won
the fight fair and square;
A Giraffe wonders;
What it's like
down there?

These thoughts are
of my own design;
its hard to compare
the beautiful chaos
of my mind.

The words I speak

My world is often askew,
With surroundings spinning
From the beginning
And tightropes moving,
Strange and confusing.

Endless negotiation
And oh, the frustration,
For...bang!
I'm down once more
I'm on the floor.

Its like trying to hang
washing on broken pegs;
Still I wobble through
on my jelly-legs.

I know I think differently
And I know it does show,
But I sing the words
That others don't know.

This is my world
With its own walls,
I pick myself up
After numerous falls.

I open my arms to everyone;
I want to make that clear
You are most welcome
To join me here.

I will give no apology
For who I am,
And I will work with what I can
To embrace the only me
And be the greatest I can be.

A discordant song

Making me stand up when anyone speaks
Is a misguided, cruel technique;
Repeating everything you say three times;
It is wrong and it crosses the line.

I know you genuinely think you assist,
But your good intentions totally miss.
It's unacceptable how it feels;
Humiliation is a big deal.

The unkind; they laugh at me
Every single time they see;
This behaviour brought to the fore;
I want to be swallowed in the floor.

So in the background I try to fade;
I learn not from notes that are made,
But again that's the wrong thing to do;
And I get pulled up in front of you.

Actually it's in front of everyone;
And the unkind have more fun.
To my note-taker I try to explain,
But she does not feel my pain.

"Don't be ungrateful" is what I'm told;
And again I'm left out in the cold.
The teacher thinks he is helping; that I know,
But I just wish that I could go.

My friend she tries to explain;
She does her best to make it plain.
But why should he listen to another child?
He's clearly annoyed, though it is mild;

Waves his hand; sends her away;
Well, today is more of the same.
I understand the way you see;
But would you like it if you were me?

Whether you read it or were given advice;
Being at this side is not very nice.
You are misguided the way you use it;
And that is why I can't read music.

From the pier

From the pier I listen with my eyes,
Today my eyes don't tell me lies.
In the distance, church bells ring,
Making my heart leap and sing.

My focus is the movement of the sea;
Its splashing swell is joy to me.
The water gently hugs a boat
That on the surface bobs and floats.
It passes through rippling waves,
Leaving disturbance in its wake.

But peaceful lapping is restored to me,
and there is beauty in the sound I see.
Whether the ocean's angry attack
Or a soothing, gentle lap;
Watching it helps to unwind;
It is music to my mind.

Genetics explained

I know that we stand apart;
We have done from the start.
One of life's mysteries that hadn't been solved;
A conundrum waiting to be resolved.
But now with an answer on my tongue;
I feel as though we have won.
For no longer in limbo do we float;
And at last we've anchored our boat.
With satisfaction I can say;
Refreshed for a brand new day;
An explanation finally,
But what you need to know is:

I am me.

The ins and outs of a lunchtime supervisor

I didn't have too many rules;
I was always firm but fair.
Tuesday to Friday they'd toe the line;
Mondays – they'd rock on their chair.

"Miss – we'll be so good"
Promise many but on the dot:
"Please WALK in the corridor!"
Bottom line – I think they just forgot.

"Don't talk with your mouth full.
Food's for eating – please don't throw";
But I taught them to use cutlery;
For some of them didn't know.

If they refused to eat:
I'd ask for '5 tiger bites';
(not of me though; of the food)
And they'd eat without a fight.

Famous for rotas I was;
Cleaning's a good skill to learn.
Most of them enjoyed helping;
When they had their turn.

I had a couple of nemeses;
Quite trying they liked to be.
They had many attempts;
But never got the better of me.

One young lady hated cleaning;
She complained about it non-stop.
When I was kind but firm;
She did it in a strop.

She didn't see why she should help,
When she could go and play.
And that little lady was tough;
She made sure had her say.

Secretly she had trained up;
One a bit younger than her.
Taught her to miss her duty
And cause a bit of a stir.

My suspicions quickly rose;
When the youngster disappeared.
And when I went to find her,
It was exactly as I feared.

In the toilets patiently waiting;
The little one was sat.
Unsure how long to stay
Before coming back.

There was a little flaw -
their plan had hit a block.
The little miss had no concept;
Of the passing of the clock.

She did miss her duty;
But both were pulled in line.
They would have alternate days,
Until there was such a time;

They did their duty happily;
Without a single gripe.
They soon saw I meant it,
And quickly earned their stripes.

When hot dinners began;
All wanted to be through.
Every child was arguing;
In the waiting queue.

Receptions first, I decreed;
For they were only small.
For the others: a rota
Would be fair to all.

Mondays were often difficult;
Especially in wind and rain.
Children had pent-up energy;
And inside they'd remain.

Wet play on pet day;
brought problems of its own.
They would get the pets out;
- I really should have known!

One Child brought a rabbit,
and put it on the floor.
I had to hurry to catch her;
Before she reached the door.

And those poor stick insects;
Probably had a headache.
That was a Monday as well -
Oh for pity's sake!

But the other days my job I loved;
Though it was bitter outside.
Strange when you consider;
The cold I can't abide.

Outdoors we were observant;
Of my whistle I was immensely proud;
And if a car came trundling;
I'd whistle really loud.

Then there was 'Foxes and Farmers';
The game they were not meant to play.
But the youngsters were so crafty;
And determined to have their way.

They'd organise games in whispers;
But I was in on it too;
For my super-power is lip-reading;
They wondered how I knew.

So Mondays and wet plays were difficult;
But Tuesday to Friday was fine.
I enjoyed looking after the children;
And helping them to dine.

Not through rose-tinted glasses

I look back and forth with cloudless eyes;
Not always kind; but I feel it's wise.

And though I choose to remember thrice;
The memories that are clear and nice,

The less happy was my time too;
It gave me tools to get me through.

I think of those times with respect;
When I look back and reflect;

For then there were more useful lessons;
Perhaps that made a bigger impression.

Just as important, maybe more so;
Is the difference in what you learn and know.

It is life's own two – for – one deal;
The bad to teach, the good to heal.

My healing place after all the damage;
With their help I learnt to manage.

At boarding school, I enjoyed my classes,
But they taught not to look
Through rose-tinted glasses.

Unknown

At the start I stand staring;
I know not what lies ahead.
Forwards is inevitable,
Sideways is not an option,
And behind me the way is blocked.
The bright dark of the unknown;
Others might join me down the line,
But I begin the journey on my own.

As I go further along the path,
The route grows ever more dim.
I entered this maze of my essence,
Became part of a fairytale of my own mind.
Inside my head I dip in and out
Of well-known once-upon-a-times;
Of nonsense fantasy,
Of Nursery rhymes.

A patchwork quilt of what I grew up with;
Here every choice is a riddle,
Nothing is what it seems.
I left straight-forward outside.
It seems unnatural
For the lights are blindingly bright,
But at least they are here,
And they give me fight.

I will follow them,
Be led by my own thoughts.
There is only me in my head;
The words of my mouth;
The hope of my courage;
The fear of my flight;
The heart of desire;
To do what is right.

Inwardly my doubt is loud,
Ear-splitting at times.
I must trust it.
I will grasp the fire,
Board a new train,
Into the woods
And out again.

The un-enchanted forest

Year one heard 'The Enchanted Forest'
it was the story of choice.
They listened with eager ears,
To the sound of the teacher's voice.

"Right" she said closing the book,
"now that you've been shown."
"You each have a piece of paper;"
"Paint a forest of your own."

She expected; pixies; fairies; elves;
But in my mind was a stunningly beautiful scene;
There roamed; parrots; lions; tigers;
Among magnificent jungle green.

But when I went to paint it,
It stayed firmly in my head;
And my piece of paper was filled
With a rubbish version instead.

Well, I was truly horrified
By what I had actually drawn.
I painted the whole page black
To cover up my scorn.

Unfortunately at that moment;
The teacher chose to appear;
For I hadn't realised that
She was lurking near.

"What have you drawn?" she asked,
Observing my page of black.
Well, straight away I answered;
Then wished I could take it back;

"It was dark in the forest" I told her,
"So dark I couldn't see."
At first I was pleased with my answer;
It seemed logical to me.

But I quickly had second thoughts;
It soon lost all its attraction.
It went down with teacher badly;
Judging by the annoyed reaction.

"Stand outside Headmaster's office!"
She said, pointing at the door.
I had to leave the classroom
Whilst staring at the floor.

Painting the page black
Seemed a good idea at the time,
And headmaster had a chuckle
When he found out my little crime!

Footsteps in the dark

As I wander along this enchanted road;
Feeling but not seeing where I go;
I know not what is to come;
Intriguing for others but scary for some.
This path is a nervous place to be
And for others it won't be like it is for me;
With twists and turns, people I've met;
It is not as I expect and yet
I trust it unlike another;
And I find I can follow no other.
My life is lit by intriguing footsteps;
Sometimes I've cowered – sometimes I've leapt;
The steps take me where I need to be;
Whether I feel or whether I see;
All will become clear in time;
For these footsteps in the dark are mine.

footsteps in the dark

In memoriam

When my earthly days are done,
My personal battles fought and won;
I promise my time will be well spent
And I'll be proud of where I went.

Tinnitus

I have a private engine of my own;
I can hear it - and me alone.
The tinnitus is right here in my head;
So I understand when it is said;
'The quiet is noisy; silence is loud'
For sometimes this noise drowns out a crowd.

Dido's equation

The teacher, he seems nice,
but he doesn't understand.
My note-taker is away today,
So I have no helping hand.

He likes to have music playing;
Specifically Dido's songs.
It is very nice music,
but the time and place are wrong.

I already struggle with this subject,
And my lack of hearing doesn't aid.
How am I supposed to learn maths
With Dido being played?

The result is when the panic
And the stress I feel, have won;
Confusion overtakes,
And the work; I don't get done.

I'm taken out and when I return;
"No drama club" he says;
For after school tonight;
I have a detention instead.

Just As I Am

He's decided I was being naughty;
I wasn't, truthfully, I tell you;
I am punished for panicking,
But what else can I do?

I felt out of my depth before,
I feel worse now that I'm in trouble.
In detention, Dido still plays,
And my head is such a muddle.

"You were just being silly before"
He tells me as I try do equations;
He doesn't explain it this time;
He did on the last occasion.

He sits and watches from his desk;
I sit and hopelessly flounder,
Until he has no choice,
But to end the pointless encounter.

If I hoped the ordeal was over,
He says sternly in that classroom of his;
"I'm not happy with you at all"
There's no doubt how cross he is.

Hearing or not

I don't know who came to the door;
But I'd never seen them before.
I don't know if they had a double chin;
I certainly didn't invite them in.

They wore an invisibility cloak,
There weren't any puffs of smoke.
They waved an invisible magic wand,
To steal my hearing and abscond;
But those intentions were unclear
Until sound faded from each ear.

Stony silence was left behind;
Like a blockage in my mind.
The invisible stranger and my hearing;
Finished their act by disappearing.
Their very presence was lost in a crowd;
Their arrival was quiet; their leaving loud.

Not loud in the normal sense of the word;
Not a huge noise that can be heard.
I opened the door not knowing what I'd lose;
And there was no one there to let me choose.
There was no prior knowledge to act upon;
It was when they'd left, I knew they'd gone.

Things then became unspoken,
For my original ears were broken;
And there was nothing to help them mend;
So silence became my very good friend.
Grown ups are aware of potential thieves,
Now I have an eye on people's sleeves;

Just As I Am

Just in case of hidden tricks,
But back then I was only six.

Now, I would not change what came before;
I don't let trials become a chore.
For I am me, Sir: Ma'am,
And I am proud of who I am.

To be clear: for my hearing I do not grieve,
But hearing aids they can deceive.
People say they comprehend,
That sounds together often blend.
What we hear can be confused,
And we feel quite bemused.
But do people really understand
Unless they've experienced it first-hand?

Deaf in a hearing world

We hard of hearing get wires crossed;
There is confusion, for direction is lost,
Then we tie ourselves in knots
And when you're Deaf in a hullabaloo,
People shout to try and get through,
Or talk to others instead of you.

Lips are important, subtitles matter;
Not turning backs to have a natter,
Or whispering, all cloak and dagger;
Background noise can be just as tricky;
An echoing building, the traffic's busy,
The wind outside, a buzzing city.

A crowded restaurant, a firework,
A phone rings, going berserk;
Behind a mask is quite hard work;
Rustling paper behind a desk,
Mishearing something and having to guess,
but that can get you in a mess.

The rain on the roof going pitter-patter,
Something dropped; crash, bang, clatter;
Or if there's just a lot of chatter.
We hear the world through our eyes,
But sometimes they can tell us lies
And we end up feeling butterflies.

Just As I Am

The silent life can be a bit tough
And information can be a bit rough;
Eyes don't always explain enough,
With many noises you can't really hear,
Spoken words are not very clear;
When an eye becomes an ear.

I don't always hear sounds like you;
Daily, the music I listen to;
Some days 30 is loud enough,
Others top volume is getting tough.

Only once in my life an owl I heard;
Well, you might think: that is absurd!
But others like me have heard it not
And I feel lucky for what I've got.
I am Deaf in a hearing world.

Ally Schofield

The power of haggis and physiotherapists

I'm different – I always knew;
I have my own point-of-view.

My thoughts will vary
in strange ways,
And each my uniqueness
Then displays.

With everyone else's
My skills are at odds;
It's unexpected,
But on I plod.

38 comes before 30
In this world of mine.
Still it has
A certain shine.

Unusual as it is...
What can I say,
It is my realm,
The version I made.

I go and see my physios
After haggis for brekkie,
They work around me
With Physio techie.

Just As I Am

They join my wavelength,
We work for an hour,
I'm full of haggis,
My superpower.

They think of all sorts
To work with my brain,
Physiotherapists,
Welcome to my domain.

The melody in me

From the moment of birth;
I belonged on the earth.
And whether I sink or swim;
I follow the joy within;
Like a song I never forget;
My very own words, and yet;
Everyday the words change,
But fit the music – it's so strange,
To my life it is the key:
It is the melody in me.

The life of a Diabetic

Teenage years are difficult;
Secondary school can be tough,
But understanding often helps;
I was diabetic, sure enough.

Sometimes I felt after diagnosis;
The truth they didn't see;
I didn't have diabetes;
The Diabetes was me.

I don't enjoy the hypos;
A cold bubble I can't break through.
Sometimes I feel like a pin cushion;
With all the jabs I do.

Now tablets introduced;
Counting I no longer do;
Carb digits messed my head;
It made me feel blue.

Blood sugars can be frustrating;
I watch my diet, at least I try;
But I can't always find a reason,
When the numbers go too high.

But there are positives here,
too - even in bad health;
For in this case if you look;
There is a kind of wealth.

It gave me a healthy diet,
And helped others too.
Healthier eating in my family;
Diabetes introduced.

I enjoy my exercise more,
And, though I get annoyed,
Occasional treats are sweeter;
I don't miss what I avoid.

I helped with a needle fear,
I had to prick more and more;
But now I have a libre patch,
My fingers are no longer sore

Yes, it can be disheartening;
No, I can't always explain,
But when I get it right;
There's much confidence to gain.

I come from an unusual place;
A 'Diabetic unknown';
I am not Type One or two;
The genetics are my own.

Along with brother of course;
Our sugars don't match the norm;
Indeed we are unique;
But we will weather the storm.

For me the pros outweigh the cons;
Though life can be hard and hectic;
Given the choice, if that was possible;
I'd still be diabetic.

My burning question

Mixed up lines;
Limbs in a muddle;
Read the wrong sign;
Ended in a puddle.

A sudden 'Wham'!
Balance is gone;
It's who I am;
Is it wrong?

Played on my mind;
The lack of the 'norm'.
A path inclined;
A gathering storm.

Do others also find it tough,
But hide it better than me?
They facilitate sure enough,
And comfortable they be.

Gratitude I can't describe;
Genetics found my condition,
The physios know my vibe,
And navigate my position.

No extra help, or so they thought;
With the news they brought.
But I disagree;
No more suspense;
Things make sense;

It's changed everything for me.

My world

I would not change
The way I am -
It's what I've known
Since my pram.

The way in which
I graciously learn
To appreciate
My world will turn.

I approach things
How I can
So I'm proud of
Who I am.

And I use
my life tools
To work with
My own rules.

I try follow them
whatever they be
To the best
version of me.

And remember –
this is true
I try my best,
and so do you.

A window into Critical Illness

I would like to dedicate the section 'A window into Critical Illness' to the amazing doctors and nurses in the intensive care unit at the Cumberland Infirmary – without whom I would not be here. I would also like to dedicate it to ICU Steps in Carlisle and my fellow ICU patients, all of whom I look on as friends – thank you for helping me in my recovery, as I hope I have helped you in yours.

My diary is dedicated in memory of both my Grandads, Eric and Peter, and my Grandma Sheila. Thank you for helping me through such a difficult time, each in your own way.

I wrote 'The angel on my shoulder' for Grandad Eric, whom I miss very much.

'A wander in Whitby' is of course dedicated to Grandad Peter and Grandma Sheila. All those holidays in their caravan in Whitby when I was little, created so many memories that I was able to draw on when I was so ill.

'There are people to help' is dedicated to ICU Steps in Carlisle, and 'There isn't a manual', to all my fellow ex-patients and their families. As alone as you feel sometimes, remember there is always someone thinking of you.

A diary of what I remember

Waking Up

Increasing bright lights pull me back to reality, persuading me to open my eyes.
I cough at the strange horizon and the tube in my throat. More coughing ensues as the young doctor on my right is talked through the removal of the unwanted contraption. There are three doctors on my left and the lady doctor among them is giving him very clear instructions. It seems to be his first time, but he follows what she tells him very well.

Immediately I'm met with a brilliantly familiar voice:

"Welcome, Ally!"

"Grandad?!" I think in amazement.

He chuckles at my surprised delight and bursts into song: "Three cheers for the girl who found her way back!"

The pristine white hospital bed seems unnatural, and my view is a blurry mess without my glasses. I wish I could get up, but I know I can't, and I'm attached to all these wires. I don't yet know why I'm here.

"Don't panic, Mr Mainwaring!" comes Grandad's encouraging tone. "You've been ill, your body needs time to heal, and to remember how it works. Don't rush yourself"

Where is my voice? And New Year's Day

I realise that I feel more comfortable without the tube in my throat and I'm more aware of myself.

I know I'm in hospital, but where is my voice? - And why can't I move my hands? Grandad said my body needs to remember how it works.

I think it's New Year's Day and Mam will later confirm it. Of course, the other thing I want to know is whether she went to church? While I can't remember the day itself, I remember that Christmas Day was a Sunday, and so New Year's Day must be too. It is difficult to make myself understood. I can't speak or make gestures with my hands, and I'm not fully in control of the shapes my mouth makes. It takes a while, but I get my message across. No, Mam didn't go to church. She seems surprised that I want to know. Otherwise, Mam and Dad sit with me and hold my hands. They talk to me a bit, but it is a comfort just to have them there. Is my brother alright, I want to know. Yes, he is. I don't really know what has gone on here. I don't remember before, but I know I must be ill. I know my current situation and though I remember very little, I'm aware that I wasn't in this room before. At first, I thought I'd fallen asleep very deeply – I do know I was tired – and maybe they moved me when I was asleep, but they took a breathing tube out, and that tells me, it is much more serious.

After Mam and Dad have gone, I think about it being New Year's Day. Where have all the days gone? It was Boxing Day, the last I remember.

"Are you in my head, Grandad?" I ask.

"Of course, I'm in your head" he responds as though it's the most obvious thing in the world - and it is, now that he's said it. It could never have been anything else.

"If you could have anything right now, what would it be?" Grandad suddenly asks.

"I would ask for some pictures of Benjy and some of Dad's Yorkshire puddings" I tell Grandad,
with a sudden fancy for the delicacy of my Dad's and the comfort my rabbit gave me after my knee operations.

"I'm afraid, your Dad isn't able to make Yorkshire puddings" Grandad explains "They've run out of milk at home."

Run out of milk? That won't make my brother happy! Pictures of Benjy flick through my mind.

"Thank you, Grandad" I say.

Visits from home

I live for my daily visits from Mam and Dad. Each visiting time, they sit and hold my hands and talk to me about the world outside the unit. The world I'm not party to at the moment. I can't answer, but I can listen. They bring me things to remind me of home and things to hold to help with the movement of my hands. It slowly improves.

Sarah from church comes to visit and she prays with me. She gives me a special cross to hold. I can't tell her, but it means a lot that she came to see me.

"I'd love to meet the Mad Hatter," I muse at one point "That would liven things up!"

"The Mad Hatter is unavailable." Grandad informs me.

"Is he having a tea party with Alice?" I ask facetiously.

"The Mad Hatter is the property of Lewis Carroll and is unavailable for copyright reasons."
He replies.

Of course, I thought it would be something like that!

"If you could go somewhere – anywhere - where would it be?" Grandad asks.

"I'd get a steam train out of here" I respond without hesitation. I'm met with silence. It was not the right answer apparently! I try again. "Whitby"

"Great idea!" Grandad says and suggests I visit the Magpie Cafe. Of course – I always do.

Glasses and drinks

The ability of my hands improve and I can finger spell. I have absolutely no voice, but at least I have a method of communication, which enables me to ask where my glasses are, and I can see again. Everyone was desperate to make sure my hearing aids worked, so I could hear, but no one realised how much I rely on my glasses.

Mam and Dad bring me in cards from home when they visit. There is one from Monkey World. My Auntie had contacted them and told them how poorly I've been. I still don't know exactly what is going on, but everyone is so kind. Our singing group at church asked me what my favourite hymn was, and they recorded themselves singing 'The King of love (the king has come)' for me. Mam brought it in for me to listen to. And Ciaran, a good friend from our boarding school drove up from Manchester to see my brother, Peter and check he was ok. Ciaran then sent a card in for me, with Mam and Dad when they visited.

My throat is so dry, but I remember the tube I had in my throat when I woke up. I remember feeling a 'pop'. I will later find out that the 'pop' was them unclipping the neck brace that held the tube in place, and that the tube was down my throat, not actually through it, But right now I don't know that and I'm worried by the gruesome thought that everyone can see inside my throat – and that water might come out of the hole. I can't tell anyone my worry, so instead I manage to communicate that I need a drink. They'll soon tell me if I'm not allowed one.

The nurses give me a covered cup of water with a straw, with the instruction that I have to sip it very slowly. I haven't been able to take solid food or drink for a while, so I mustn't rush myself, no matter how thirsty I feel. Mam helps me sip a little, and later a little more before she leaves, then to my dismay, the water is placed out of my reach.

A while later when a nurse comes to check on me, I communicate that I'd like more water. I'm given it but told again to sip slowly. She comes back later to take it off me, but I keep a hold of it. She says I can keep it with me but is worried that I will pour it over myself, as my grip still isn't that good. I keep an eye on it, moving my hand upright again if it tilts. I will sip it slowly but I'm
stubbornly determined to keep the water with me. No one is going to take my water!

You're supposed to be looking that way

Another nurse comes on duty. I spend most of my time looking to the right in the direction of the other patients – simply because I have so many wires on that side of my face, attached to a machine. My neck muscles are weak and though I would like to look the other way, my neck is not strong enough to fight with the pull of the wires. Every time I look to the left, my head is soon pulled to look back the other way. The nurse doesn't like it – at the time, I think that maybe she thinks I'm being nosey and staring at the other patients. I'm not. The whole time I'm locked in my head with my own imagination and not seeing them. I find out later on after I've left hospital, that she might just have been worried about me kinking the tubes and wires. Anyway, the nurse comes over and directs my head the other way. Every time she goes off and my head is pulled back the way she doesn't want, she is back again:

"You're supposed to be looking that way." she informs me briskly.

I have no voice to explain to her that I have no choice because the wires are pulling my head the other way, so what can I do?

"If you see her coming over, turn your head to the left. Even if it is brief before you get pulled back again, it might be enough to put her off!" Grandad suggests.

"Oh, why couldn't I fall down a rabbit hole or go through a wardrobe to Narnia?" I lament.

"As I explained, Wonderland is the property of…" Grandad begins.

"Lewis Carroll" I finish.

"And Narnia is the property of C.S. Lewis." He continues.

"Yes, yes - copyright." I sigh "but it would have been interesting!"

"Look, the nurse is coming back" Grandad warns me.

I obediently turn my head to the left and do my best to continue to face that direction. Out the corner of my eye, I see to my relief that it works. The nurse nods at me and walks away.

Will my voice come back?

The other nurses are lovely though and when I'm up to it they help me to have a bit of a wash. I get very tearful one day during the wash, frustrated that my voice is showing absolutely no sign of returning. What if it doesn't come back? What if I have to find another method of communication for the rest of my life? And will I ever be able to sing again? I love singing. It would be a great loss to me. I manage to get across to the nurse that this is what I am worried about.

She is very comforting and explains that often when you have a tube down your throat, it causes a bit of damage which needs time to heal, but it will in its own time.

"We're communicating ok, aren't we" she tells me encouragingly. "I can understand you. Try not to worry."

"She's right" Grandad says afterwards "It will come back. I'll make sure"

I feel a bit better.

Up in the chair

"Would you like to sit up in a chair today?" I'm asked to my delight.

Yes, I would. It's progress, isn't it? Mam and Dad are delighted to see me up, though I still have to wear an oxygen mask. I do realise that I would quite like something to eat, but I still have worries about food coming out the hole I still think is in my throat. I can't ask, so I wait for someone to suggest it. If they think it is alright, it must be. The water didn't come out anyhow, so maybe the hole has healed up? I enjoy my first lunch when I finally have it, although, I find I need to take regular breaths in between mouthfuls to start with. After that I have food every mealtime.

A view from a fish bowl

I get introduced to the astronaut helmet. It reminds me of a fish bowl. I struggle with claustrophobia, and I don't like the look of it. They say, if I can have it on for a while each day, it will improve my oxygen levels more quickly. I really don't want to, but I can't explain and yes is easier to communicate than no. Surely, I could grin and bear it for a while? And I'm known for 'trying things', so I nod.

It turns out to be much worse than I thought. When it's put on my head, I feel like I'm being stabbed with pins and the little air I have is trying to be dragged out of me, as quickly as the helmet is putting it back in. I want to shout, but I can't.

"You can do it, Ally. Just hold on." Grandad tells me.

I keep trying, because I know the nurses are only doing things to help me, but my neck muscles are so weak. It doesn't take long for my head to droop, like a little child's rag doll. It's my hypermobility rearing its ugly head again and the awful aching swiftly brings on a migraine. It quickly intensifies the more my head hangs. What if my brain turns to soup?
I try to explain to someone about the migraine, but I can't whisper never mind yell and I can't make myself understood at all. They say they know the astronaut helmet is unpleasant, but that I mustn't worry.

I've reached my limit. I'm desperate for a break, however short, from this migraine, the aching of my neck and the claustrophobia, but every time I manage to silently beg to be let out for a bit of respite at the very least:

"Another few minutes" I'm told "And then we will let you out."

This is the worst claustrophobia I've had. The panic suddenly grips me, like someone has pushed a button. What if I never get out? The terror brings me to tears, though part of me knows that it's silly. These are lovely people and they're trying their best to help.

They can see my distress and they try to calm me down. I do my best to – but my best isn't good enough. The panic gets worse not better and when it does dissipate a bit, it soon comes back.

Is this how a goldfish feels? I don't ever want a fish in a bowl. I couldn't put a fish through this. I will finger spell that to Mam and Dad later.

The panic comes over me again and the migraine is still increasing. My neck hurts from being lax.
It can't take the weight it's been given.

But this game I can not lose. After all, I need to help my oxygen levels.

"Remember what you do in MRI scans" Grandad suggests.

Well, I don't have an eye mask here, and the helmet is much closer than the scanner would probably be. I can see everything I don't want to see, but I have my other methods. They might work. I try to recite the books of the bible in order, then I try singing 'Shine Jesus Shine' in my head.

It works in MRI scans, but the problem here, is the migraine. It's so bad and it stops me being able to concentrate. I can't focus my mind at all and despite my best efforts, the claustrophobia takes over again. I want to shout:

I HAVE TO GET OUT!

But another trial hits me - I haven't walked for a while and my legs have sort of forgotten how to, so to run away is not an option. I wouldn't know where to start with taking this helmet off anyway.

At last my message seems to get through.

"This isn't working for you, is it?" A nurse says. Somehow I manage to shake my head "Ok, we'll find something else." she agrees.

The astronaut helmet is taken off. I experience both physical and mental relief. Next, they try the c-pap. I am going to do this, because I couldn't bear to be back in the astronaut helmet.

"Grandad, please help me through this." I silently beg. "Just don't let them put me back in that thing."

"I won't" He promises.

A blunt reminder

I wear the c-pap with no problem, but I can't help being relieved when Mam and Dad arrive, and I'm allowed a normal oxygen mask instead. I finger spell my experience of the astronaut helmet – or the fish tank as I call it. They agree that we will never get a fish. They leave after my tea arrives. I am helped back to bed and eat my tea, then a doctor I've never seen before arrives.

"You are not doing well enough." He states "If you don't improve, we will have to sedate you again. We don't want to, but we won't have a choice." Then he leaves again.

"Did you understand what he said?" A nurse asks me as I stare after him in shock. I nod. It was perfectly clear.

It hadn't really hit me how ill I'd been until then, and up to that point everyone had been telling me how well I was doing and giving me encouragement, so it came as a real shock, but it was what I needed to hear.

"I have to pull myself together." I say to Grandad. "They are NOT going to sedate me again. My family and friends have been through too much already."

"Molehills, not mountains, remember" Grandad points out. "You can do this."

"You know that c-pap mask reminds me of Whitby," I tell him "The air and the spray off the North Sea."

"That's a good idea," he agrees "you know Whitby like the back of your hand."

I want the c-pap on

I manage to catch the attention of a nurse and communicate that I want the c-pap mask back on. I spend the evening in it. I don't mind the mask anymore. I have Grandad and I spend the time exploring the Whitby I know and love in my head. I go to Robin Hood's Bay and Scarborough a little bit as well. The only thing is, it does tend to dry my mouth out, so before bedtime, I have a short break to have a drink and then it's back in the mask to go to sleep. I get woken up a bit later and told I have to have it off for a while, to give my face a break. That's ok with me, I don't mind either way. They bring me a carton of apple juice. I had rather a fancy for it and Mam and Dad brought me some in. They brought me in sugar free chocolate mousse too, when I started eating again – and a home-made chocolate truffle – a staple of a Schofield Christmas.

Why won't they let her sit down?

I remember one of my aunties – Mam's sister, coming to see me. She had an argument with some of the staff and I remember Mam telling me:

"They won't let her come back!"

Then Mam walked my auntie down to the car park, but the next thing I knew my Auntie was next to me.

"Your Mam has had a bit of an accident and has dislocated her ankle, but don't worry she is in the right place. She's in A and E. They are just sorting her out, then she'll be back here with you."

I couldn't understand why no one would give her a chair when she visited, after that!

I kept wanting to tell her: "You shouldn't be standing! Sit down!", but I had no voice to do so.

Mam's chicken korma

"I wish Mam could bring me in some chicken korma" I say to Grandad, when it suddenly crosses my mind.

"I doubt it's the first thing on her mind at present" he points out "Besides it might be a bit messy!"

I imagine bright yellow sauce accidently dripping on the pristine white hospital sheets. Ok, that is a fair point.

My days in the c-pap

For a while, I mostly spent my days and nights in the c-pap mask – having little breaks here and there, when I have a drink and then wear a normal oxygen mask for a while. My Diabetes consultant Dr Fathima comes to visit me a couple of times, while I'm sat in it, although I can't really see her very well because wearing the c-pap doesn't allow room for my glasses. Eventually, I'm told I don't need to wear the c-pap overnight anymore, just a normal oxygen mask.

A couple of days later, I am mostly on the normal oxygen mask, with only very short stints of the c-pap if my oxygen levels aren't coping. Eventually, I come off the c-pap altogether.

Our vicar, Graeme from church comes to visit me. It is very encouraging to see him. Of course, I still have no voice and can't speak to him, but he talks. I listen and he prays with me. He asks what my favourite hymn is.

"The king of love (the king has come)" Mam tells him on my behalf – knowing that's the hymn I asked for from the singing group. Graeme says he will put it in his next Church newsletter for me.

One morning, I wake up and the same nurse who had been in the day before is in again. She says, 'good morning' and 'would I like some breakfast?' I answer her with my voice – I don't know who is more surprised – me or her!

"There you go!" Grandad said "You didn't need to worry. Your voice came back"

Mam and Dad bring my phone in with them on one of their visits, now that I am able to move my hands. This proves to be very useful as it enables me to read the texts my Mam has sent to my friends about what's happened to me. I read them that night so I understand more than I did and this morning a doctor visits me.

"Do you understand where you are and what has happened?" He asks.

"I'm in hospital" I reply and reel off that I've had flu, Diabetic ketoacidosis and pneumonia. I will later find out after leaving hospital, that I've also had sepsis. The doctor seems satisfied with my answer, however.

Later the physio visits me again. So far, we have done mostly breathing exercises and walking on the spot. The bottom of both my lungs have collapsed so I have to work to reinflate them. This morning, to my delight, she helps me walk around the room I'm in. I send a text to Mam telling her and Dad this but keep quiet about getting my voice back. It will be a nice surprise later.

My brother is coming to see me this afternoon, which I'm looking forward to. He has an appointment downstairs. He will come in with Mam, as I am only meant to have two visitors at a time, then Dad will come up and collect him. Dad will then come back and join Mam and I, after delivering my brother to Audiology.

"Hello," Mam says, when she and my brother arrive.

"Hello Mam" I answer from the hospital chair. The response is as expected. She is delighted. "You've got your voice back!"

"It was there when I woke up" I tell them.

After a while, Dad comes up to collect my brother. It was lovely to see him. Then Dad comes in to take his now vacated space by my chair:

"Hello Dad" I say.

He is just as delighted.

How could I put them through this?

Now I am able to talk, I can ask questions and voice my thoughts. By the time Mam and Dad leave, though they did their best to play down their own distress, I'm in no doubt, exactly how hard things have been for them.

I keep the knowledge to myself until they have left, but that evening the guilt hits me like a truck.

"How could I do that do them" I ask my on-duty nurse. I don't remember Christmas, but I do remember choosing not to tell anyone exactly how unwell I felt, in case it spoiled Christmas. I'm now aware that my decision nearly killed me.

The nurse comforts me. "It's not your fault" She assures me. "Your family and friends are ok. They are happy you are getting better."

"She's right" Grandad agrees. "It's going to be ok."

I'm ten times more determined now, to put this behind me.

Black figures on blue

Being able to speak for myself also enables me to ask about memories I have. I am given a diary the nurses are filling in about my time on the intensive care unit. It might help me understand things that are in my mind, they explain.

Things are clearer to me after reading it, but it doesn't explain some of the memories.

"There's this memory" I say to the nurse "I see black figures, with a blue background. They move almost robotically and then suddenly stop and go back to the start – like one of those wheels that you can only turn so far before it meets resistance, and swings back again. It reminds me of a computer program or something. Do you have any idea what it could be?"

The nurse doesn't but says she will think about it and let me know if she has any thoughts. Later, she suggests that maybe the blue might be the hospital curtains.

When Mam and Dad visit, I'm glad to see her being given a chair and I broach the subject of her sister visiting, and her dislocated ankle. No, my Auntie wasn't here. She wanted to come straight away, but Mam asked her to stay where she was and make sure Gran and my Auntie D were ok. As for the ankle, Mam did break a toe accidentality kicking something, but that is all. It's later explained to me, that patients who've been critically ill and have been in a coma, can suffer from this sort of thing – delirium they call it.

Cricket

"I wish I could watch some cricket" I lament to Grandad.

"It's not the cricket season over here." He points out. No, it's not, but I still wish I could watch some!

A nurse offers later to bring in a tv so I can watch some football. As usual, there is a match on.

"No, thank you" I tell him "But I would love to watch some cricket"

He loves cricket too and says he would happily bring me a tv to watch it if it was the right season or they had Sky in the hospital. Instead, we have a conversation about the Ashes.

My Aunty asks my age

On a number of occasions, a group of doctors come around the unit, discussing each of our cases. One doctor out of the group will introduce a patient and then if that patient is able to communicate the doctors might speak to them or ask them questions. At first, I had no voice, then I had a c-pap or oxygen mask on, so for now they haven't spoken directly to me, other than saying they hope I feel better soon. It's one of these doctors who reminds me of my age. Up to now I was convinced I was 37, but of course I'm not. This proves useful, when I later receive a text from my Dad's sister, who has been debating my age with their brother. My auntie thinks I will be a certain age on my next Birthday, but my uncle thinks I will be a different age. He has apparently all but convinced her she is wrong, so she is rather pleased to find out that she is right! What I don't admit to at this point is that if my aunty had asked me yesterday, I wouldn't have had a clue what the real answer was. Now I know, thanks to those doctors!

I often get visits from the hospital chaplains. They come most days to talk to me and pray with me. It means a lot and I know Grandad is as comforted as I am – that was something he often did, and it was a very important task to him. Now that I have my voice back, I can talk to them too. I introduce one of them to my favourite hymn, which he hasn't heard before. He finds it on the internet using his phone and we listen to it. He seems to like it, and I feel I have 'done my bit' in sharing it.

Sausages

Now I can speak, I can ask for the breakfast I'd like, instead of just nodding or shaking my head when I'm offered something. Before it was cereal and water. I have a strong desire for sausages.

They don't offer cooked breakfast in hospital I'm told, not that it's a surprise, really. I opt for toast, orange or apple juice, a glass of milk, and a cup of tea.

Night Writing

The nurses here are lovely. One night we have power cuts – there is a storm outside. The nurse on duty comes over to me to check I'm ok, when the lights go out.

"It's ok." She says "It's just a power cut. You're safe." She stands by my bed, until they come back on, to make sure I'm not frightened.

During another night, I wake around 3am with poetry in my head. I'm always afraid of forgetting it and I know I won't sleep until I've written it down. When I'm at home, there is normally a notebook by my bed for such occasions, but I don't have one here.

I call the nurse on night duty over and explain the problem. She doesn't bat an eyelid. She goes away and comes back with some paper and a pen, helps me to sit up and puts the lamp by my bed on. Then she leaves me to it.

I haven't written for a while, so it is even less neat than normal, but I get about three or four verses down and am satisfied I can now sleep. I text Mam in the morning and ask her and Dad to get me a notebook and bring it in when they visit later.

You need another line in

One evening, I'm told that I will need another line put in – in my other arm. It is used to take blood more easily while I'm in hospital. The current line in my right arm is no longer working. It isn't a surprise to be told, as I watched one of the nurses struggling to get any blood out earlier, but it is not a pleasant thought. I remember very little from before I woke up, but I realise I'm aware that they found it very difficult to get a working line into me in the first place and it required a number of goes to do it. The second line is put in my left arm, and is also unpleasant, requiring multiple goes.

I later get an infection in my cannula, which also has to be replaced and put in my other hand. It works for a day or two and then it also becomes infected. I can painfully feel every drop of saline or antibiotic that goes through it. I have a third cannula put in – this time in the arm that no longer has a line in it and it is much better.

You're eating better

The doctors who come around talking about cases, have got into a habit of arriving when I'm eating my lunch. They are very apologetic about this, but one does tell me on the Friday, that I am eating better than earlier in the week. That time, I was having to take a breath, between every mouthful, but now, as he points out I am able to eat normally.

I can talk to them now. My on-duty nurse hangs around though, to make sure I hear and understand any questions I'm asked.

A bad night and a breakdown

During that night, I am extremely uncomfortable and can not sleep. I call the nurse over and it turns out there is a problem with the catheter. I am so embarrassed, although the nurses are all lovely and tell me not to worry, but I have a very bad night as a result and am on the emotional side on Saturday.

The nurse who comes on duty in the morning is informed in the handover that I have not slept well, so I am left to lie in for a while. It is later discovered in my daily blood tests, that I have a bit of an infection lingering around my body. It probably adds to the lack of sleep and the events in the night and doesn't improve how I feel. On top of that, I was told yesterday that they were considering moving me from intensive care to a normal ward. Last night it was good news, and I was excited about the progress I was making. It was one step closer to home. However, in the cold light of day, after a bad night, moving to a ward, where I have less easily obtained assistance, should I need it, is a very daunting prospect.

"It's ok, Ally." Grandad says.

I sternly tell myself that I need to pull myself together, but I still feel mortified about last night and am now panicking about the move, so when Mam and Dad visit later, I can't stop the tears falling, no matter how many talking-tos I give myself. I feel worse when they've left, because I must have worried them again, but sometimes you can't help crying, and the warmth and care of loved-ones acts to induce such tears.

Off to the ward I go

I do manage to pull myself together later and the antibiotics they've put me on soon target the infection. My move has been postponed at the moment, until the antibiotics kick in.

"Molehills, not mountains" Grandad reminds me gently. "It was a blip, but you're fine now."

On the Monday afternoon, I am finally ready to go on a normal ward. The physio arrives at the end of Mam and Dad's visit. He walks me around the whole intensive care unit and when we return, the bed I am to be taken on is ready. One of the hospital chaplains sees me on my way and I am touched when he tells them:

"Look after this one – she's special!"

I eat some tea when I get to the ward and have one of my cartons of apple juice. I am also given a cup of tea. There are a few other ladies on the ward with me, most of them elderly. One is a similar age to me, though she isn't on our ward for very long. When a nurse comes to see me to give insulin later, I tell her that I'm not sure how things work on the ward. She explains that I have a button to ring when I want something. I am also visited by a nurse, who tells me she is there to check on my transition to the normal ward.

My time on the ward

I'm ok on the ward. They are very nice, but of course there is less assistance, as I was told. I finally have the catheter removed the next morning, which is another step along the road. In the mornings, we wake up and are given breakfast, followed by having our curtains pulled round so we can wash and dress – though it is just a clean nightie. We get another cup of tea or coffee late morning and the others on the ward all watch the little tv's attached to their beds. I don't want to slip into 'a daytime tv' routine and have got Mam and Dad to bring me in some puzzle books and some monkey world magazines. Then we have lunch, followed by more of the same, sometimes broken up by visits from a doctor, a nurse or a physio, or someone similar. About two or three pm, another tea or coffee is offered and visiting time. Our evening meal is between four and five, and later we get another cup of tea or coffee.

My mind gradually grows accustomed to being a bit more independent again, but there are a couple of frustrations. One is my blood sugars. My insulin and tablets are locked away for safety reasons. I have to ring my bell and wait for someone to come and take my blood sugar reading, before I can consume the meal in front of me. Consequently, it is probably not as warm as I would like it to be when I eat it. I have to ring my bell again to ask for my insulin, which I am meant to have straight after my meal, but sometimes on the ward it can be anything up to four hours after. My insulin was with the nurses on the Intensive care unit, but my blood sugars were monitored more closely, and I was always given it straight after I'd eaten. I have no control here and I know my blood sugars will not improve until I am home and allowed to administer my own medication again. The other frustration is that I can not walk to the toilet on my own. I have to ring my bell, as I still have to hold an arm to walk and am currently attached to an oxygen tank, which is heavy and requires someone to carry next to me.

Homeward bound

I am told by a doctor who visits, that I will remain in hospital while I am on oxygen but will be allowed to go home once I am off it. I am gradually able to downgrade my oxygen masks, as my levels improve, until I am allowed off it altogether. A nurse visits and takes some blood from me. She has a little trouble finding some. A physio also visits me and gives me a stick. He helps me walk around the corridors.

On Thursday, a doctor visits. He says they think I am ready to go home. I text Mam and relay this with instructions for clothes she can bring, along with coat and shoes. I also ask them to bring my stick, which we bought when I had an injury as a teenager and has remained in the loft since. It is the same as the one the physio gave me, so I can leave the hospital's stick here. The second line was taken out on the unit, before I came to the ward, but a nurse comes and removes the cannula in my arm. My arms and hands are black and blue!

Mam and Dad arrive later, and the doctor comes back to check I'm happy to be discharged. He goes away to talk to the diabetes team on the phone, while Mam helps me get dressed, and Dad goes downstairs to bring my coat and shoes, and a wheelchair. While Mam and I sit waiting, the doctor returns and tells me that the diabetes team would like me to stay in hospital another night.

"But if you really want to go home" The doctor says "I'm not going to stop you. I'm happy to discharge you" He must have seen my face fall!

"I'd really like to go home." I tell him, trying to phrase it politely, despite my obvious disappointment.

"I'll go and call them back." He answers.

Dad's face also falls when he arrives back with the chair, but it is ok. The doctor returns and tells us that the diabetes team have agreed I can go home. We just have to wait for my medication to be sorted, and forms to be filled in and signed.

Back in my abode

It's so nice to be home and I enjoy a toasted cheese sandwich for my tea. It is a little odd being in my own bed at first. For a start, my body has trained itself to wake up during the night. In hospital, a nurse would come around and do blood tests, take blood pressure readings and that kind of thing. Every time I wake up now, my brain thinks:

"Am I allowed to go to the bathroom on my own, or do I have to ring a bell? - Am I still attached to wires or oxygen?"

I do suffer nightmares the first week or so back home – deep down I am still worried about the hole in my throat, but a conversation with Mam and Dad teaches me that the tube, that up to now I thought went through my throat, didn't. It was just down my throat, and I learn the 'pop' sensation was the neck brace being unclipped, when the tube was pulled out. I no longer have nightmares after that.

It does also go through my mind on the first night home:

"Have I done the right thing? What if I'm not as well as I think and I put everyone through heartache again?"

"Don't doubt yourself" Grandad tells me "You are doing brilliantly. And coming home was the right decision for everyone." And he's right.

I was given the choice of what dinners I'd like on the weekly menu, the night after I'd come home. What did I choose?

Cumberland sausage, Mam's chicken korma and a roast with Dad's Yorkshire puddings of course!

The corridor to heaven

While my body sleeps,
My mind has walked for days,
But I feel strangely undepleted,
In every possible way.

This corridor, highly illuminated;
With each step becomes brighter still.
One foot in front of the other;
It's as easy as going downhill.

All around I feel warmth;
How long will I be here?
It is a place of comfort;
Those who left me feel near.

Onwards there is only good;
I know that – I just know.
But a sudden pull of my heartstrings;
And further I can not go.

For there will be no going back;
My heart knows this is wrong.
And a voice informs me of just that;
"Go back where you belong."

It tells my aching heart;
"You really shouldn't be here.
It's not your time so return
To those you hold so dear"

I turn back without hesitation;
Though some I love are ahead.
Most remain attached to earth;
I must be there instead.

I wish to run but I find;
I only reach snail pace.
In front of me the way is steep;
But I know it's not a race.

So patience I try to practise,
Not a mountain; just a molehill.
Slow but steady on I travel,
For I know I have the will.

A marathon and not a sprint;
And though dormant my body lies.
My mind is open; I'm on my way;
And I will open my eyes.

The harrowing frost

It happened in winter; a world of fragile things,
But there is still life and birds still sing.
Another beginning, not the end,
The freshness of cold has hope to send.
I am with you though I am asleep,
And when I wake your hearts will leap.

Stay behind

I had angels at my feet, they whispered in my ear;
"The way is blocked; you shouldn't be here."
Death met me before my eyes:
'Not now, not yet,' she hears me cry.

I knew nothing of how or why I was there,
But I did know that this wasn't fair.
She tried to beckon me across the line,
I was not ready; it was not my time.

I have more to offer and much to gain,
and I must try to soothe their pain.
So back I go; I will turn around,
And I won't stop 'til I am found.
Giving up is not something I understand;
I will greet the cold of winter with both hands.

Ally Schofield

When you wake up in hospital to a mute, blurry view

I can't find a bridge to cross the moat;
Couldn't find water if I fell out of a boat.
I have to get used to a blurry place;
Can't see what's staring me in the face.
To see details I have no key;
I can't see what is in front of me.

My perspective is vague – does it show?
Can't see past the end of my nose.
Is it raining? I can't check;
I'd rearrange chairs on a sinking deck.

Can't see the wood for the trees;
Well, I can't see the trees actually.
This view of things is not my choice;
What would I say if I found my voice?
Something that would put me at ease...

Can I have my glasses please?

My sewing box

My Christmas embroidery box,
Hit the bottom; was on the rocks,
A stringy jumble, a mass of threads,
A confused clump, a muddled head,
A swirling labyrinth, a tangled mess,
A complex puzzle, a place of stress,

Each individual colour was me,
But the point of it I couldn't see.
The big picture; it made no sense,
And sadly caused me great expense.

The knot got bigger,
The puzzle thicker.
And much greater,
As big as a crater.

For I'd kept a quiet voice,
In the end I had no choice,
I had to go and see the seamstress,
Ask for help to sort the mess.
To have much needed alterations,
There were too many complications.

It wasn't enough,
I felt so rough.
And still the knot grew,
Til' it blocked my view.
I'd kept a quiet voice,
Now I had no choice,

But to go upstairs
All hope in prayers.
For a higher opinion,
In their dominion.
Enter the knot,
Where time is lost.
I was in the grip of defeat,
The waves knocked me off my feet.

I started to rise after the fall,
But then I had no voice at all.
The new seamstress did excel,
Brought me back from my farewell.
Worked away at the knot,
And gave me back such a lot.

Singling out each little thread,
Clearing out my muddled head.
Each different colour laid out aside,
And I rose with the rising tide.
Each problem I had they sorted out,
Til' I could laugh and I could shout.
Until the single threads of mine,
Brought together a new design.

They lay there on their own,
Singular but not alone.
And the vital seamstress,
Such heroes; the very best.

Just As I Am

They started again right from scratch,
And helped me to win this match.

The threads I have don't join each other,
Each one is separate from another.
For too much time since has lapsed,
I've gone so far that I can't go back.
But no longer in a tangle are the threads,
No more muddles inside my head.
Each new day I happily greet,
My sewing box is tidy and neat.

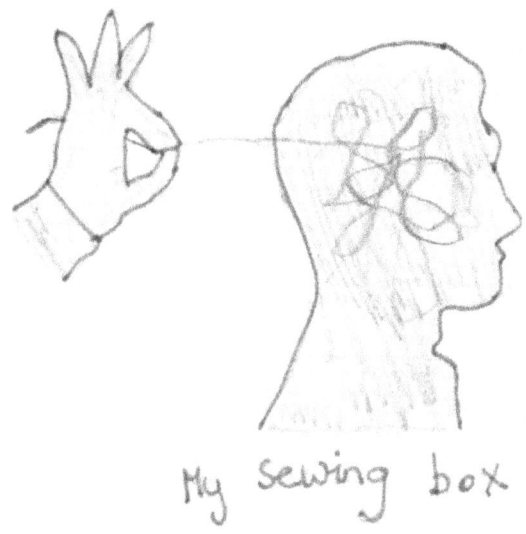

My sewing box

The door is closed; the house is empty

Rat-a-tat-tat;
No answer to that.
Impatience stamps on the concrete,
For there is no one here to greet.
Nerves cruelly scrape the gravel,
For they don't like having to travel.

But the knocking is unanswered still;
Locked outside in the chill;
All my emotions here remain;
To stand hunched and share the blame.
But there is no one awake here,
For things have stepped up a gear.

A forced slumber is upon me,
I really had no choice you see.
It was a case of 'nothing or this'.
So for now I have to miss
Real life for a little while;
To stop an illness so hostile.

It should help me on my way;
Please do try another day.
And just to be perfectly clear;
Then I definitely will be here.
My arms will be open to welcome in;
Every friend and every kin.

My emotions will be unexposed;
But for now the door stays closed.
Everyone is welcome in my abode;
Where prayer and love freely flow.
Whilst family and friends; they are plenty;
For now this happy house is empty.

The angel on my shoulder

My world had turned upside down
As I lay in my hospital gown.
With my voice unable to speak,
All I knew was out of reach.

Stay with me please, I silently beg,
But visiting time was at an end;
Communication like blood from a stone,
So there I was left, all alone.

But I had the angel on my shoulder,
Then it felt no longer colder.
For Grandad whispered in my ear,
And I felt like he was near.

The angel on my shoulder

The hauntings of an induced coma patient

They looked in my eyes, but there was no one there
For of my surroundings, I was not aware.
My exhausted body succumbed to forced sleep
and when they tried to wake me, I was in too deep.
They tried to keep my condition steady
Until the time when I was ready.

When at last my hibernation was at an end
There was a lot of damage left to mend;
The tube in my throat was a shock
And one of the first things I came across.
'Take it out, take it out,' I beg in silence
For I had no choice but to be compliant.

My hands didn't work, my voice didn't exist
And then I found out what I had missed;
For a while had passed since I last knew,
I heard the date, but it couldn't be true.
Time has been lost; where have I been?
What happened to the days in between?

I couldn't tell what was real or what was not;
In my muddled mind, there was such a lot.
Did my auntie come and see me?
Mam hurt her ankle – or did she really?
I heard an argument, it didn't make sense.
Tubes, tubes, tubes, from a bed with a fence.

And the most vivid haunting that I had -
Black shadow on blue - doesn't sound bad
But the way it moved, unnatural with a jerk.
Strange, like it was not of this world
And I just couldn't get out of the rut,
Repetitive, like when a record gets stuck.

But really haunting were words so blunt
which weighed on me heavily, like a ton:
"You're not doing as well as you need to be."
Threat of relapse, pain of friends, of family.
Everyone gave encouragement, love, and light
But sometimes someone needs to tell you to fight.

The ballad of an out-of-reach life

I woke from a deep sleep,
Not knowing I was me.
It should have been a cheerful day.
But I was still at sea.

The bright lights attacked like punches
With the clarity of mud.
Before I know the guilt is there
It hits me with a thud.

I'd travelled through the dark,
On my journey home.
People were all around,
But I was still alone.

Though they took the tube,
The silence still was mine.
Everything seemed wrong,
I failed to reach the line.

For now stop the clocks,
They mean nothing; time or day.
The past would not have happened,
Had there been another way.

My mouth will not form words;
I have some questions you know.
The thoughts in my head are stuck,
They have no where else to go.

I look up at no sky,
I look around at sea.
Distant land, are you there?
But there is only me.

Each visiting time would come,
When my hands in theirs were clasped,
But my paws; they remained useless,
My mitts; they would not grasp.

The smiles I recognised,
Hour on hour as I lay.
What's the point in asking why?
And I can't anyway.

And what of outside?
I can't ask anyone you know.
Is there a patter of rain?
Or a light dusting of snow?

I know winter still dominates,
And the festivities already left.
I remained in their hurry,
And I feel a bit bereft.

So I imagine the sky,
The blue unclouded weather,
But the light is unnaturally bright,
Like candles burning together.

Just As I Am

Now back inside my head,
Warm sun rays fall on me.
The salty refreshing spray,
Of the desolate forlorn sea.

I'm told I'm doing well
And hopefully winning my fight.
Then his words come out of the blue,
A sword in a cloud of light.

But now my hands; they work,
On the bad I must not dwell.
My mind grows ever more sharp
And now I can finger spell.

Push back I must, when I see
Shadows of the world appear.
The road home is faint,
But the riddle becomes more clear.

Rough terrain on a dark night,
Is the road I have not taken.
If you see this as the end,
Then you are much mistaken.

I will ride these waves of lifeless sea,
The laid out miles of strife.
I'll meet with land once more,
And bring this ocean to life.

I sail the sea for days in my head,
Wishing, hoping, and then;
Three cheers I say; land ahoy!
For my voice is back again.

A view from a fish bowl

An astronaut helmet they called it;
Some new and clever kit.
I thought it was more of a fish tank;
Did I fancy it?
Not really thanks.
It looked to me like a 'mare;
In normal circs; I wouldn't dare;
But my oxygen levels are low;
So I will give it a go.

The small space caused great panic
And I felt waves of manic.
My weak neck gave me pain
And my eyes started to rain.
The migraine was so intense;
That was causing great expense.

So they gave me the c-pap instead;
And I roamed Whitby in my head.

A View from a fish bowl

Oxygen masks

I'm losing breath and I'm shaking
Don't want to make the fuss I'm making.
I tried to block out the fear
To see through the falling tears;
But my head aches and I want to shout:
"Someone please get me out."
The feelings come in relentless waves
And I'm struggling to be brave.

With a different kind of mask,
It feels quite the task.
For the situation is unbelievable,
But it is still achievable.
I'll breathe through this frustration,
And use imagination.
I'll focus the mind and clench the fist,
And start my journey through this mist.

I'll keep pushing a little bit more;
Until I reach the open door.
I've been to Whitby a million times;
I know by heart all these lines.
So the negatives I'll just ignore;
I'll get back where I was before.

Bet on it

The astronaut helmet, I couldn't do
A plastic sphere without a view;
It felt like I was in a fish bowl,
And though I tried with my heart and soul;
The claustrophobia was very real;
Such panic it made me feel,
My head hung when my neck flopped,
My breathing was wrong; the fish bowl was stopped.

Everybody was talking; saying I was doing ok,
But one had something else to say;
"We don't want to go backwards but you need to improve,"
"If not; back is what we'll have to do."
Thought I; 'No way'; I understood what he said;
'I've got to get on my positive head',
'Can't have this again; more of the same',
'My family and friends don't deserve the pain',
'I've got to listen to my own heart talking',
'I've got to start my mental walking',
'Not climbing a mountain; just a molehill',
'I can do anything with enough will',
'The staff saved me; gave me help from my bed',
'Now I need to count on myself instead'.

So with the c-pap, I made my peace,
For it reminded me of my beloved Whitby;
A place I know like the back of my hand;
Then I knew there's nothing I couldn't withstand.
In my head I explored Whitby as I pleased
And indulged in the North sea breeze.

Just As I Am

I escaped to Scarborough and Robin Hood's Bay;
Thanks to so many family holidays.

Have you lost yourself to protect others more?
Did you ever get on a ride you never wanted to board?
Stayed too quiet to the people you hold close?
Made those mistakes, because you just didn't know?

How do you know the right path to take?
Should I question every decision I make?
The machine breathes for me; again their hearts break
I don't ever want to repeat these mistakes.

Did you think you were right till death nearly came?
Then realised you were wrong though no one was to
blame?
I will savour each and every day;
and through this, I will find my way.

You can count on me;
Just wait and see,
I'll get better and I know how;
I'll turn things around and I'll start now.

I won't give up – that's who I am;
I'll give it all I've got; that's my plan,
And I will find the strength; you know I can;
Will it take time? Quite a bit.
Will I get there? Bet on it.

Determination

I couldn't get it out of my head -
That shocking thing the doctor said;
I knew I needed to step up the gears;
I put in blood sweat and tears.

I'm on the edge of ok and not;
But I will give it all I've got.
I'll make it happen now I know the drill;
Don't tell me I can't - believe me, I will!

A wander in Whitby

Transferring from warm sand I set forth,
to the icy deep waters of the north.
A sharp intake of breath escapes my lips,
And the pit of my stomach does a flip.
It's cold, but refreshing with the smell of salt,
And in my tracks it makes me halt.

As I move away from the salty chill,
Past little voices excited and shrill.
Children entertained with buckets and spades,
Some in the sun, some in the shade.
Riding on donkeys and eating ice cream,
A treat that makes their faces beam.

I move into the town: there's so much to process,
I smile to myself and wonder at its busyness.
The whiff of fish and chips reach my nose,
Well nothing says Whitby quite like those.
Hunger awakes in the pit of my tum,
I tell myself I must go and get some.

Oh that smell of the magnificent Magpie,
A building that soon catches the eye.
Memories of Grandad Eric it brings,
Where we would sit and eat like kings.
It was the cafe that he always chose,
So there we'd queue and there we'd go.
With his 'why am I waiting' sense of humour,
His voice of good song; a tuneful boomer.

Ally Schofield

From the window I watch happy and free,
The gentle reflections of the shimmering sea.
But the harbour waters are tempest-tossed,
As the lifeboat enters with the calm now lost.
It passes by the great and small,
guarding lighthouses, short and tall.
Still formidable; devoid of duty,
Old and wise; but things of beauty.

The waves crash carelessly on the land,
Back and forth; dragging the sand.
Breaking an otherwise silent atmosphere,
A sound I love; though I can't always hear.
I avert my eyes from the ship,
Long enough to savour my fish and chips.

I wander through the old town on the east side,
Leaving for a while the rising tide.
I set foot in the fishermen's domain,
The cobbled streets that still remain.

Past Sandgate's, our fish shop,
Many delights to make you stop.
In there I pop on my way,
To find the flavour of the day.
 Cockles, mussels, Dover Sole,
Or further on I take a stroll.
For there in the old smokehouse wait,
strong smelling kippers for your plate.

The next bit is too much for some,
To the 199 steps I come.
A place where the passing time it shows,
Always the same number, but each one grows;
For each step got smaller as I got bigger,
The time on them gets ever quicker.
Easier than ever is my long climb,
I reach the top in next to no time.

And there in front is a ruin of old,
A place once grand but still so bold.
Each brick worn and weathered by strife,
The feelings, the turmoil it's had in its life.
This is Whitby, a place that is dear,
Somewhere that brings me the greatest cheer.

A place that continually evokes,
Grandad Peter; all his jokes.
It was his most favourite place,
I see him there in that space.
I think of the many conversations,
We had on those special occasions.

How he wiggled his ears to make us laugh,
Oh we had a time and a half.
And his favourite joke,
He'd share with us folk;
Laughter is medicine; he was quite right,

'My teeth are like stars'...
'They come out at night'.

The strange thoughts of
a patient's muddled mind

The unnatural light
seemed overly bright;
For this meeting
It shouted a greeting;
At my muddled mind;
And I woke to find;
I'd been near extinction.
This harsh distinction;
From what I was used to;
The normal I knew;
Like those shocks;
When your insides drop;
Suddenly hit the floor;
And you feel raw.
It suddenly occurred to me;
How lovely it would be;

If hospitals were purple.

The road I didn't tread

I did not put on my best coat;
Nor my hat and shoes.
Instead I wore my slippers,
And returned to what I knew.

For the gates themselves were pretty;
They had a certain gleam.
But I missed my city,
Whatever could it mean?

Voices I loved I could hear;
So I returned back home.
They were all so near;
Saying "you're not alone."

The way I had to find;
It all happened in my head.
But with joy I left behind,
The road I didn't tread.

The road I didn't tread

Ally Schofield

Since the Christmas that didn't happen

I feel it in my bones;
Life has a different tone.
To sing I have every reason;
I love the feeling of this season.

Sherry; scrabble; Carols at King's;
So much joy that programme brings.
Then I will enjoy my Christmas dinner;
The home-made truffles are a winner.

I will sing carols one and all;
Hang the holly: deck the hall!
So many hearts I will gladden;
Since the Christmas that didn't happen.

Sometimes you need to shout

Keep calm and keep going,
On and on I'd march.
Stumbling forward blindly,
Through each towering arch.

I would walk and walk,
As though I could see.
press on when music fled,
and fade into the trees.

I did not wish to be a burden,
on those I really love.
Nor the bringer of bad news,
To the people above.

But it is a bigger lesson,
Than any other I've learnt.
I learnt it the hard way,
And got my fingers burnt.

So if your candle wanes,
Dig deep and find a flicker,
Make sure someone knows,
And you get help much quicker.

Because silence can be deadly,
believe me it is true.
Sometimes you have to shout,
To keep on being you.

A birthday almost denied

Nature is a true marvel,
And I almost met my fear;
Stars would shine without me,
And I nearly wasn't here.

Beside a lake today,
In this beautiful glade,
Gathering swallows twitter,
And they'll never fade.

I sit under the trees,
Though I can't really hear,
I imagine the crickets singing,
Lap up the atmosphere.

Oh it's such a blessing;
The burnt orange sky;
The magnificent setting sun,
Will always catch my eye.

I sip tea nearly not drunk,
From a flask nearly not used,
The appreciation hits me,
I feel deeply moved.

I do not sleep, I am awake;
There is no need to cry,
So I drink in and savour,
A Birthday almost denied.

The spark

My very core shook;
With the advantage nature took.
My condition was very weak;
Relief my brain did seek;
To rest my body broken;
Till strength was re-awoken.
A door slammed in my face;
But it left an empty space;
A lot of words unspoken;
A window blowing open.
It told me I could cope;
That little bit of hope.

So in the dark;
When you think you're done;
When heavy rain clouds;
Eclipse your sun.
Search the sky
For a hidden star;
Guide it to you;
Near or far.

Let its rays warm your heart;
All you need is a little spark.

There are people to help

Life was harsh and overtook,
Your inner core it really shook.
What happened was so complex,
Where do you turn to next?

When things get on top of you,
People are around to talk it through,
The nicest people you could meet,
Will give you support; help you defeat;

The demons you have; big or small,
So when you feel you've hit a wall;
Please remember you are not alone,
It may feel like you've kicked a stone;

But sharing it can give you a break,
With troubles it left in its wake.
When you've been in intensive care,
Things can feel hard to repair;

But these people catch you when you fall,
They're all around - and there for all;
For it leaves behind many effects,
Come and talk to ICU Steps.

There isn't a manual

There's no one to choreograph this dance;
So please give yourself a chance.
There's no sommelier to match wine to this meal,
And your own recovery is a big deal.

No weatherman can describe this forecast,
Try not to think of the past.
There's no thermometer this temp to gauge,
But it helps to work with just one page.

For there's no clock to tell the time,
And no deadline to finish your climb.
There's no calendar to give you dates,
And you don't need to juggle plates.

Nothing can say when this tide will turn;
Be gentle with yourself; don't be stern,
And if you are struggling along a bit;
Remember no seamstress can make this dress fit.

No bell will ring when dinner is ready;
The best way is slow and steady.
There is no gardener to tend to your flowers,
And don't work in weeks, work in hours.

For this direction there is no compass;
For every achievement blow your trumpet.
There's no map to tell you the move to make;
So be proud of every step you take.

It's not as simple as treading a line;
Everything will happen in its own time.
No one can tell you the right way to feel;
There isn't a manual to explain how to heal.

There isn't a manual

Where my heart is

I want to dedicate the section 'Where my heart is' to my brilliant family and friends. You all mean the world to me. 'University days and ways' is written for Jackie Sibley and Carol Kenny, great friends of my Mam's from their university days, and now they are my friends.

'Strength inside' is written for my Auntie Doreen, one of the internally strongest people I know.

January

In Sparkles, January speaks,
With biting fingers of glittering frost,
Breath floating and rosy cheeks,
Scattered leaves that winter tossed.

Hibernating little frogs
Long past the night of Scottish Burns
And spiky gentle sleeping hogs
Waiting 'til the warmth returns

February

In short, February narrates,
Bitter Jack nipping a nose,
A month of love the freeze berates,
Fennel, birch, and the primrose.

The time of the joyful chickadee,
And Feb celebrates Candlemas,
On its way out the cold should be,
As winter months finally pass.

March

In Nature does March tittle-tattle,
While celebrating a mother's care,
Hope and fortune join the battle,
Sunny daffodils everywhere.

Endurance and cheer robins evoke,
Enchanting ash tree, healing willows,
The Alder's courage, wisdom of oak,
 A new beginning the spring bestows.

April

In humour does the April fool jest,
Unbreakable diamonds gleam,
The enduring mallard minds her nest,
The Lord is raised; our faces beam.

The innocent daisy, loyal and pure,
The sweet pea full of gratitude,
Mint, rosemary, safe and sure,
Butterflies flutter in multitude.

May

Fair May is badger's address,
And the strong elm's domain,
Green emerald of success,
And plenty more to gain.

Oh lily of the valley,
Sweet nightingale sing,
Flowers of Hope don't dally,
In the throes of the Spring.

June

June boasts the glimmering pearl,
The strawberry moon does rise,
Honeysuckle twists and twirls,
Rejoice fathers being wise.

Summer brings new charm,
Dragonflies propel and water flows,
Among gentle lavender calm,
The month of the sweetest rose.

July

In July, the monkey explores,
Showy water lilies gloat,
The majestic eagle swoops and soars,
Listening to the wise old oak.

Larkspurs catch a wandering eye,
Motivating rubies shine red,
Gentle peace doves in the sky,
The winter woman long since fled.

August

Hours of study culminate,
With strength to persevere,
Now no longer do you wait,
In August, hope is sincere.

School holidays at their peak,
Hovering over meandering shiny,
That gentle, soothing, rushing streak,
A bright kingfisher, blue and tiny.

September

The ninth month does talk,
Oh yes it has its story,
The powerful loyal soaring hawk,
The Aster and the Morning Glory.

It marches its drum, it will thrive,
Balance and harmony sail the yacht,
When September does arrive,
I know you will forget-me-not.

October

Pumpkin month doth sing,
Graceful swan, quiet dormouse,
The tiny bat beats its wings,
Shy red deer, ivied house.

As dark and cold draw nigh,
Oh, hardy mountain sheep,
Autumn colours catch the eye,
Again the hoggie finds his sleep.

November

The loyal wolf is there to guide,
Penultimately red poppies remember,
This month does its best to chide,
Reflection is prominent in November.

Mugwart renews us to fight a battle,
Thyme gives us courage to try,
Booming fireworks fizz and crackle,
We celebrate the souls in the sky.

December

The elder tree of diminishing light,
O what peace and quietude,
The holly breaks into night,
And narcissus brightens the mood.

Pretty robin, insightful ravens,
A mystery with much to discover,
We snuggle in our cosy havens,
'Til winter lifts her dusty cover.

The war of Jekyll and Hyde

I am the house – I'm Dr Jekyll.
New people arrived and they settled;
I love them here but they took my crown.
Then up he rose when they knocked me down,
Bricks and mortar, stone by stone,
In he came and took my throne.
For now I have another side:
Introducing Mr Hyde

This old game he thinks he'll win,
but there are higher stakes within
And I've had years, our bonds secure,
I know I'll win - he's immature.

Though every move now lifts the cost,
I'll gladly roll – and he has lost.
Here before, I won this long ago,
But there are things that I don't know.

He thinks he'll triumph from the start,
My age sets me apart.
I'm in control, my fortune's won,
Victory's mine - I won't be outdone.
But he's brand new, they're different times….
And I've read the rules between the lines.

He said he was invited - I said what?
He answered he was chosen - I was not.
He said these people asked him here;
I asked them, just to be clear.

From where he's standing, I was left behind
And maybe this I should keep in mind.
The old part of me was knocked right down,
They well and truly knocked off my crown.
He was welcomed here instead;
Modern perks from feet to head ,
Things that work, day and night,
He offers comfort and delight.
Times move on, that's how it goes,
And from the ashes up he rose.

So think of it a different way;
I should be happy, not dismayed.
I should celebrate old and new,
He's not instead – he's welcome too.
So let's agree, join the same side,
Then we both can keep our pride.
Instead of game of Cat and Mouse,
Jekyll and Hyde are both the house.

Slap it on the plate

I want food, not art,
So I don't want it neat.
Rustic suits me fine,
I just want to eat.

Don't painstakingly prepare,
No need to take your time.
Does a lion demand elegance,
Before he goes to dine?

Don't give me a pretty picture,
I eat with my mouth not my eyes.
I see no point in a tiny dot,
So make it a decent size.

Don't swish vinaigrette or pesto,
Across the bottom of the plate.
And I'd like a real utensil,
Not a piece of slate.

Whatever you do don't puree it,
It really is a waste;
I'm an adult who likes to eat,
And savour every taste.

Please give me proper sauce;
Or a jug of nice gravy will do.
There's nothing wrong with 'old-fashioned';
Don't worry yourself with jus.

Make it as messy as you like;
I'm quite happy to wait.
Quenelles don't matter to me;
Just slap it on the plate!

The shipwreck

The shipwreck lay abandoned and cold,
But it held many stories still to be told;
In her dwelling she was sad and rusted,
And her metal groaned as the wind blustered.
Her framework threatened to separate,
And her structure had taken a beating of late;
The waves pummelled her with their fists,
But sometimes she lay sunlight-kissed.
She offered a treasure trove for explorers to seek;
Each footstep they made gave a welcome creak;
To the ship there resting all alone,
And the more they discovered, the longer they roamed;
Until, over time her body dissipates,
And in the sea, some disintegrates;
Until only the engine is left there to mope,
Useless, abandoned and still without hope;
There steadfast where her misfortune led;
On the ragged rocks, this ship made her bed.

The Shipwreck

To light the way

As the years pass me by, I stand proud and tall;
I spy the secrets the salt waves proffer.
My lesser brother signals from across the water:
Size matters not with the guidance we offer.

In raging storms and choppy seas;
I see that ships no harm can meet;
For sometimes gentle, sometimes rough;
The north swell swirls about my feet.

In autumn, coloured leaves drop but out of reach;
I am untouchable from their gesture.
November brings fireworks with pretty lit skies;
But the winter can be a chilly adventure.

The wind bites and my old bricks freeze,
But in March, blossoms bloom and fall;
Their responsibility ends when summer arrives,
And the job I do outlives them all.

I watch beaches fill with bodies and laughter;
The donkeys enjoy their daily strolls;
Back and forth with children atop;
Maybe a swim in the sea for the bold.

Sand castles, seaweed, salt-washed rocks gleam;
I see buckets, spades and melted ice cream;
Cries of 'eat your chips! Seagulls are swooping!'
Passersby greet me and with pride I beam.

But only the gulls if they are brave enough;
Share my all-year wondrous view;
They too, watch boats and yachts making choices;
The narrow harbour, squeezing through.

The lifeboat risks all: courage my special friend;
We have your back; listen to what we say;
Fear not, my brother and I are always here;
After sundown our eye will light the way.

The smell of kippers

From Fortune's smoke house where kippers are hung;
Beautiful aromas waft; wild my senses run.
Down the paved roads fishy fumes gaily sweep;
Indulgent, strong, and far they reach;
Eau de kipper, long the scent lasts;
Treating me to glances from my times here past.
This welcoming greeting with my nose meets;
As if the kippers themselves swim down the cobbled streets;
The wonderful whiff with me stays;
Bringing thoughts and memories cascading my way;
Whether I sunbathe, in the sea have a dip;
Or sit on the pier with my fish and chips,
And gliding and swerving the seagulls swoop;
Surveying my lunch with a gleeful coo;
They drop down for my crumbs because beggars can't be pickers;
Nothing reminds me of Whitby more than the delectable
smell of kippers.

Heather and bracken

As pretty as a picture in sun or shade,
Sometimes a black cloud breaks,
but don't rain on my parade.
For a shower can add more delight;
A drink to grow more new life;
A bed of heather; the odd bird feather,
Ornamental thistles, which sometimes prickle
Bracken that crackles; a challenge to tackle
The smell of wild flowers to enjoy for hours;
The baa-ing of a sheep; terrain that can be steep,
The distant chugging of a steam train,
But the tranquil atmosphere brings peace again;
From the chaos and stress of normal life;
Joy in fear; calm in strife,
The soothing breeze of the wind;
Bees buzz; butterflies flutter; birds will sing,
The North Yorkshire Moors offer everything
A feast for the senses; sound, smell, sight,
O the joy of heather and bracken in dappled light.

Abbey proud

The abbey projects a statement of old,
Up on the cliff so valiant and bold;
To stand there fearless through struggles and all;
Watching gazing minds as they enthral.

Advertising strength: communicating determination;
Tranquillity for, contemplation.
Overlooking the sea, it knows not of her rage,
And though a ruin, it's mighty proud of its age.

Once home to St Hilda, many troubles has it seen;
It holds its stance among the lush grass green,
Weathered and tired, each stone has its own story to tell;
Of the storms it has stood above the ocean swell.

Still Whitby's heartland, still upright and proud;
Still there to attract an almighty crowd;
A lesson of endurance from the Abbey: take stock;
It boasts the biggest victory for it beat Nature's clock.

Creatures of the night

Darkness falls; 'tis a whole new world;
A new state comes forth; shadows unfurl;
The creatures of the night bring mighty wonder,
Beautiful to see; they are great in number.

The daylight animals take a backseat,
a flat-tailed beaver and his webbed feet,
Just one of the many dusk will bring,
A shy roe deer, a nightjar sings.

A mammal sees the world upside down,
The chirping cricket's echoing sound.
Soaring , the magnificent screech-owl cries,
Weaving through the marbled sky.

The moon like filo pastry before it's cooked,
The cunning fox comes out to have a look,
The leopard gecko with his amazing toes,
 the digging badger with his stripey nose.

Trees wave like light never went out,
A wild boar with his long narrow snout.
The prickly marvel, out she heads,
When the winter woman goes to bed.

Just As I Am

Buzzard's silhouette against looming giants,
She gives a haunting shriek of triumph.
A smiling, whistling two-toed sloth,
A stream bursts through the undergrowth.

For even the nocturnal must quench their thirst,
In Moonshine or a damp cloudburst,
When shining Miss Moon and her daughters,
beam down from high on swirling waters.

And glassy reflections glisten bejewelled,
Or Jack frost is bitter, biting and cruel,
The wind might rush complaining it's cold,
But the night creatures out there are very bold.

Spring cheer

I regret that February and I are no longer friends;
For the time being our companionship ends.
By him I sadly feel betrayed;
By his forsaking nature: the decisions he's made.
He was meant to take the frost with him but left it behind,

And leaving the trees bare; that was unkind.
But my cold hands warm your heart;
Heat and I for long will not be apart.
A statue like I am is not very nice,
But the promise of new season melts the ice.

On a new brighter beginning we must focus;
A sea of snowdrops: of the crocus;
A wilderness of tulips; of hyacinths;
An atmosphere tranquil is our medicine.
An expanse of daffodils; a field of bluebells;
Beauty that offers the sweetest smell.
The song of birds in the trees;
A boost most needed for the lonely;
A spring in their step she will provide:
Rejoice for spring – she has arrived.

Autumn's coming

A strange object
on my flushed face falls,
In autumnal song,
the male robin calls
In yellow and red
and orange and brown,
Leaves and acorns
lie all around

The absence of green
irritates the wind,
Too soon is evening,
the light is dimmed
Pine cones lay strewn;
 Conkers can be found
The wind's rage throws
all to the ground,

Within a heartbeat
his whistles are cold,
This is a season
meant for the bold
Outside, damp and coolness
come to my mind
The winter plants grow
and begin their climb

Ally Schofield

As smells of harvest's end
hang in the air,
Time for the pumpkin,
cabbage and pear
Birds twitter,
nestling close beside,
Hedgehogs are getting
ready to hide

The animals and I think it looks stunning
But they know, what I know: Autumn is coming.

Autumn's Coming

Storms

For a while the wind has raged
And life we know had to be caged.
People batten down the hatches;
Barricade doors, fix their latches.

The gusts are cruel as ever
And some storms they can be clever.
The Lady tempest she will clasp
Every last thing in her grasp.
With that evil glint in her eye;
Beneath the moody heavy sky.

At times it might rain or sleet,
Slowly darkness in will creep.
The angry wind will blow a gale;
Crying out a sordid tale.

Oh yes, it will blow a hoolee;
Toppling over yours truly.
And shudder violently will the trees;
At a view only they can see.

Unforgiving as ever is this winter;
Though each storm is just one splinter.
Title of harshest season it claims;
Nonetheless it's always the same.

But when the wind and rain are steady;
My ruby shoes are at the ready.

153

Mother nature

This is a time I breathe new life;
I will help to relieve your strife.
Savour the fresh and gallant wild;
The smallest things will make you smile.

Otter pups, fawns, little lambs bleating;
Feathery friend, sing-song greeting;
Birds nesting, new growth blooming;
Frogspawn, springtime looming.

Sleep time over, animals reawaken;
Sudden movement – a hare will hasten.
Snowdrops, daffodils, flowers budding;
Swans pairing, peacocks strutting.

It really is beauty renewed;
I feel rejuvenated, what about you?
The natural world grows and thrives;
This is the season I feel alive.

Then they come, the long days of summer;
They can rain or be a stunner.
It can be dull or humid and muggy,
But children laugh, happy-go-lucky.

It's no-school time and they are free;
Playing games and climbing trees.
Delightful sounds that make my heart soar;
Delicious picnics, barbecues galore;

Just As I Am

Sausages sizzle, burgers blaze;
Ketchup, Ice cream, lemonade.
To shed a tear I have no reason;
This is solstice, my happy season.

Crackles and pops, sparkles and pumpkins;
A time when people make assumptions;
Many think my life is finished;
Indeed they see me as diminished;

But I have more to offer inside;
And for the people I will provide.
A period of harvest and maturity;
Autumn boasts changing obscurity.

Food is gathered, bright colours burst;
Time to dance for all I am worth.
Scarlet and crimson, russet and amber;
Gamboge, maroon, my very own glamour.
My trees put on their technicolour coat;
My carnival season is all I had hoped.

Then comes the time after the fall;
The unkind season when I bare all,
But I tell you that I still have a heart;
I give you good food and a new start.

A jolly season brings a spell;
Nothing like the fresh winter smell;
The merriment of Christmas dress;
Family, friends and love expressed.

Though some get lost in barren land,
And they might need a helping hand;
A time of goodwill and of peace,
And for others a time of sleep.

The winter can be harsh and cruel,
But there's still gentleness in the Yule.
Freezing beauty, but see through the cold;
The wonder of nature, there to behold.
A fragile world, but it copes;
Winter reminds us there is always hope.

Then my life cycle starts anew;
The ice lady fades; spring breaks through.
I have a new beginning up my sleeve;
For I arrive when I leave.
Mother Nature is well prepared;
I am always...and everywhere!

The beauty outside

Snowdrops open, this world to see;
The winter frost begins to flee.
New life grows when flowers fade;
Spring is a masquerade.

Blossom sprinkles the ground asunder;
The branches grow a green kind of wonder;
The air fills with the buzz of the bee;
Summer is a jamboree.

As the wild wind blows, autumn colours bloom;
Pumpkins cackle and fireworks boom.
The chill arrives as harvest sows;
Autumn is a magic show.

The bare trees wave against the burnt orange sky;
The frost on the dropped, wet leaves lie.
The nights grow long and the daylight lesser;
Winter as always, is a fiesta.

Through summer heat
and winter freeze;
I see beauty in the trees.
Blossoms bloom
and loose leaves fall;
The beauty outside
is there for all.

The Beauty outside

The hedgehog

After a lengthy deep freeze;
The long missed beauty did awake;
Wiping the crustiness from her eyes;
She emerged from her dream-fuelled state.

The old woman who brought on winter;
This day had long since froze,
And now that she melted with the cold;
The beauty breathed fresh air, exploring with her nose.

She pushed the undergrowth to clear her path,
And searched the lighter night;
To satisfy hunger and quench her thirst;
She used her nose for sight.

'Twas 24 hours past, since from deep sleep;
The spring sunlight kissed her awake;
She explores and drinks, and drinks and eats;
Now wide awake from her winter wait.

To the deep the beauty will return,
And she will not venture out to look;
Till winter's end, the beauty sleeps;
When the winter woman brings forth her icy foot.

The buzzard

High above the party bickering;
The dazzling splendour swiftly swoops;
A scorning glance upon the wing;
Below at the masses in their groups.

'If only you could see what I see;
Appreciate the enchantment of nature;
The beauty of being free;
Your happiness would be so much greater'
She cries; contentedly.

Eerie and haunting, at her leisure;
Graceful and courageous;
Bird's eye view advantageous;
The grandeur of this reigning treasure;
The freedom she has – her daily pleasure.

This thing of beauty fiercely mocks us;
High in the sky, with a loud taunting cry;
Over the road-worthy metal boxes;
The magnificent buzzard soars and glides.

Dressed in black

There was a time, mam;
When I didn't feel calm.
Right and I wouldn't get along;
My past was all wrong.
My world was full of setbacks,
And I was dressed in black.

There was a time, Dad;
When I knew good or bad;
Some days I'd be content;
Sometimes full of torment;
From the life I'd led,
And I was dressed in red.

There was a time brother;
Failing to read one sign or another;
The hard way we were shown;
We'd barely jump the hurdles thrown;
Because life could be mean,
And we were dressed in green.

There was a time uncle;
Life was a mysterious crumple;
Back and forth, to and fro;
No idea where to go;
It was a vicious circle,
And I was dressed in purple

Just As I Am

There was a time auntie;
I knew not what was handy;
I couldn't join the dots;
I'd tie myself in knots,
With my mind I had a quarrel,
And I was dressed coral.

There was a time Gran;
My world was lonely and sad;
Then love and light lit my sky;
I was secure; my spirits high;
My family broke through,
I wasn't dressed in blue.

There was a time cousin;
I had the full dozen;
My way unobstructed;
The road reconstructed;
I knew what to do and think,
And I was dressed in pink

There was a time friends;
I realized my purpose again;
My heart is light;
My mind is bright;
The future can unfold,
And now I'm dressed in gold.

There is a time, my family;
My life again has clarity;
The path of delight;
As long as I have you, I'm alright;
If I fall, you have my back;
I will never be dressed in black.

There is a time, my Lord God;
You've shown me the path I trod;
You taught me the road was clear;
And I'd always feel you near;
I feel content and so much fuller;
My life is every colour.

University days and ways

Dear Jackie
our great friend,
happy thoughts
we all send.
You ended up
Back in the day
At the college
On Val's way.

It is a mystery
economics
and history,
Well, I wouldn't have a clue
But I'm so glad Mam met you
And of course the lovely Carol,
Meeting up for dinky do's,

I will never forget
our trips to Oxford,
When all of us met.

Strength inside

A diamond is pretty and as hard as a nail;
A yacht moves more smoothly with wind in its sail.
A bird means freedom, though it's small and fragile;
Knowledge is more useful when you've had it a while.
A delicate butterfly represents change;
A crow can be magical, though it seems a bit strange.
Music brings with it a sense of calm;
Small objects can be lucky charms;
A coin, a horseshoe, a four leafed clover.
An olive branch smooths things over.
A key can open a window or a door
And give you a new journey to explore.
Objects have hidden meanings, making them significant,
Individuals have qualities that make them magnificent.
I know a lady who is so special and kind,
A force to be reckoned with, if ever you did find.
Her mind of steel I've always admired
And not to give up I am inspired.
Very few I know have the determination amplified
And inner strength my Auntie Doreen has inside.

Christmas dinner

Think of Yule logs before you slice,
For Yule logs are feeling blue.
Though they taste very nice,
That's only to me and you.
Think of Yule logs before they're scarred,
They say 'to eat us would be a pity.
'we're made with lard, our icing's not hard,
We can sit on the table and look pretty.'

Think of mince pies before you tuck in,
Their short life is sadly doomed.
Sitting on a shelf for months is grim,
Just to be taken home and consumed.
Think of mince pies, they're very sociable
In a box of a dozen,
They say all emotional,
'it was awful in the oven.'

Think of cranberries; don't eat them for supper,
They do their best to try and hide.
Let them be: don't make them shudder,
They cry when you take them inside.
Think of the cranberries; I'll keep it short;
 They say 'Please show us some care.'
'You'll turn us to sauce for your main course'
'And poor turkey. This is unfair.'

Think of mulled wine, give it a chance,
It used to be fruit, my dear,
In a vineyard in France, those grapes used to dance,
To music only they could hear.
Think of mulled wine, don't dine.
They say 'Please let us quietly sit!'
'To go from the vine, to be festive wine'
'Is an occasion we'd like to miss.'

The Christmas pudding has earned a lot,
For ages she has sat and matured.
Figgy or not she doesn't like being hot,
And must flambéing be endured?
Oh I know the figgy looks good,
but they say, covered in sauce,
'We feel drunk from the brandy which is not very handy,'
'When you're trying to be an elegant last course.'

Praise him

The section 'Praise Him', is dedicated to my church family back in Chalford who helped bring me up so well, especially Shirley Bushell, and to Brenda Cox – thank you for organising the forest walks, which I really enjoyed, and my open-the-book team. And to my church family at Holme Eden – thank you for being so welcoming to us and you all have a very special place in my heart.

It is also dedicated to someone very special: thank you God for being my constant.

To all the staff I worked with at Oakridge Parochial School, and those working there now, thank you for supporting me with my poetry – I really enjoy writing a new poem for the school every year, and all the Christmas Poems are dedicated to you as a thank you.

'To sing a while' is written for my amazing music group at Holme Eden, thank you for asking Mam and me to join and let's keep on making beautiful sounds!

Where my faith leads me

Where my faith leads me can be a brick wall or the way through;
Moving north was a great choice – not that I knew.

Where my faith leads me can be a shot in the dark;
But on new chapters, one must embark.

Where my faith leads me can be winter or spring;
But a voyage of discovery the decisions can bring.

Where my faith leads me can be a glass empty or full;
I'll never get anywhere wrapped in cotton wool.

Where my faith leads me can be a sheep or a lamb;
For the lessons I've learnt - glad I am.

Where my faith leads me can be a window or a door;
But I am better equipped than I was before.

Where my faith leads me can be a trickle or a fountain;
like a distant view of snow on a mountain.

Where my faith leads me can be a puddle or a lake;
Life can be difficult – or a piece of cake.

My path I shall follow, happy or sad,
For my faith has given opportunities
I might never have had.
Where my faith will lead me
Sometimes I do not know,
But the faith in my heart teaches me
Where I need to go.

To sing a while

This is comfort in a song
A tune of hope when things go wrong
Musical medicine plays its part
Joy for every longing heart

Those whose journey now is hard
Those who need to travel far
Who tread the rocky path of life
Those who hope with all their might

Bid my anxious fears subside
Give shelter for fragile lives
Voices to plead the cause of the meek
For those who are afraid to speak

In rough waters, make them brave
Keep them floating above the waves
Through sufferings and future fear
Whisper courage in their ear

Music take them to another place
Let them find love and grace
The dried up stream once more will flow
The withered plants again will grow

Clear their minds to give them chances
Here the questions come with answers
No more tears, no more pain
Let them see there's hope again

Just As I Am

Give them freedom from the toughest
In this music find healing comfort
That never lets their hearts grow cold
Gives them time to take a hold

The strum of a guitar, a thundering organ
To help the release of their burden
The stroke of a keyboard, a drumbeat of hope,
To help them feel that they can cope

Craftman's art and music's measure
The sound of music is our pleasure
Our melody we raise to bring a smile
Join with us to sing a while.

No more dominion has this death

A special supper, Bread and Wine blessed;
A home within a wilderness.
A garden of tears, a treacherous kiss;
That led to a road such as this.
No more dominion has this death;
He died, He rose, to give us breath.

A heavy cloud on Friday descends;
For us He came to make amends.
Hear angel armies of the sky;
On that cross he went to die.
No more dominion has this death;
He died, He rose, to give us breath.

To have his innocence nailed down;
To wear forgiveness like a crown.
God proclaimed the just reward;
For us sinners his love out-poured.
No more dominion has this death;
He died, He rose, to give us breath.

Our Lord laid in a lonely place;
He broke the chains of our disgrace.
The shadow of a mighty rock;
The three-times crowing of the Cock.
No more dominion has this death;
He died, He rose, to give us breath.

Just As I Am

Our many sins have led our way;
For we like sheep have gone astray.
Now all is covered in sorrow and gloom;
For Jesus is placed in the tomb.
No more dominion has this death;
He died, He rose, to give us breath.

Disciples grieving and forlorn;
But such Joy brings the Easter morn.
Now the cross and passion past;
bright morning here has come at last.
No more dominion has this death;
He died, He rose, to give us breath.

Sing Hosannah, Fling wide the gates;
To celebrate we can not wait.
He banished the heavy clouds away;
He changed earth's darkness into day.
No more dominion has this death;
He died, He rose, to give us breath.

Death no more Dominion has

Lest we forget

We give our thoughts
to those who were lost,
For never once
did they count the cost,
They fought with bravery
of the utmost,
And the courage they showed
at their post,
Is something none
will ever forget,
And we will always be,
in their debt,
We give them special silence
on the hour,
And a proud remembering
Poppy flower.

Each year, we will
always remember,
And honour the noble
in November,
The fallen will forever
 have our respect,
Every one of them:
For lest we forget.

Nestor's story

It is time for me – a donkey called Nestor
To tell an amazing tale of a special year
Of Wise men and shepherds full of mirth
Angels singing of an important birth

A braying account of my story
When I welcomed here the king of glory
The wind was bitter with little moonlight
When I carried Mary through the night

In Bethlehem there was a biting frost
Mary needed a room, at any cost
But to no avail Joesph appealed
Until one innkeeper, at last revealed

'I have a stable warm and dry
A place to shelter, from the sky
A hay filled manger, a crib for a bed,
In there the little one can rest his head'

The cattle were lowing, I recall
I proudly stood guard in their stall
The son of God born under my gaze
And sweetly sleeping in the manger laid

Up on the hill, a most beautiful noise
A chorus to the shepherd boys
A glorious host of angels singing
Words of joyful tidings bringing

Wise men travelled - they came from far
On this dark night, they followed a star
Before the precious child they bowed down kneeling
Gold, frankincense and myrrh revealing

As Joseph and Mary - the mother mild
The Shepherds, the wise men in awe of this child
Like the angels, the star in heaven above
I tell my tale with wondering love.

A Nativity shared

On a bitter winter's night,
Surrounded by a glowing light,
Ivy in her rocking chair
Spoke the words she had to share.

Tell to all, each year she would,
A wondrous story of news so good,
To many children and their friends,
Spreading Hope which never ends.

Children listening round the fire,
To Ivy, a lady they did admire.
They gathered on the patchwork rug,
Each with hot chocolate in their mug.

All would come from far and wide
To sit and listen by her side.
Her voice, accompanied by sounds
Of instruments played all around.

Each grown up had a music device
To match the words so concise;
While the Mums rocked and swayed,
All the Dads rattled and played.

Ivy, a lady so wise of years,
Shared the knowledge that was hers;
All engrossed round about -
The roaring fire faded out.

One cold eve so long ago,
Very draughty in the snow,
It was bitter through and through,
There was a maiden, dressed in blue.

Mary was in a wearied way;
She'd travelled far with donkey's bray.
With Joseph minding the heavy load,
On they went along the road.

For Mary soon was to bear a child,
Though she was so meek and mild,
To Bethlehem they had to go;
Alas for them, the pace was slow.

Inn after inn: 'No room,' they say,
And now the baby is on the way.
Finally shown pity: "Stable's back there,"
A sweet baby born, gentle and fair.

Up on the hill, a beautiful noise
Startled some sleepy shepherd boys.
It silenced even the lamb's loving bleat
While the men turned as white as a sheet.

But hosts of glorious angels sing;
Such good news to men they bring.
"Fear not," sang the angelic choir;
Their voices just got higher and higher!

"Fear not," "Fear not,"
"Fear not" "Fear not"
The men were shaking on the spot!

Those young men left their startled sheep,
Stumbled down the hillside steep.
Their own short journey they undertook;
For the baby they just had to look.

In stable so lowly, yet full of joy,
Mary was seated, cradling her Boy,
In awe and wonder the shepherds stood round;
The baby was sleeping, safe and sound.

A wise men trio followed a star;
With their presents they travelled so very far
To go to a stable, mean and cold,
With such a wonder to behold.

There they knelt on bended knee,
Presented gifts, wise men three,
Frankincense, myrrh, princely gold,
In that borrowed place, as told.

Shepherds and Angels,
What a glorious sight
Wise men and camels,
Oh calm of night!

Well worth the donkey's tiring plod,
For Jesus is born, Son of God.

Ivy's voice echoed around,
Accompanied by the joyful sound;
A band the mums and Dads had formed.
By now all were thoroughly warmed.

The doorbell rang – an elf was there:
"I think," he said, "this is unfair."
"I missed the story," he muttered crossly,
"Can I have a cup of coffee?"

Each with a warm drink in their hand,
Supported by the local band,
Raised their arms high and tall:
"Merry Christmas one and all!"

The shepherd's tale

Some men were shepherding up on the hill
When angel song broke through the still.
The host was bathed in shining light:
"Fear not!" they announced that bitter night.

The angels, dressed in zebra onesies,
Sang: "There are no greater times than these!"
They joyfully sang of a special birth;
 The baby would save men on earth.

When the shepherds stopped seeing stripes
Two quickly mounted their quad bikes.
They said: "On the back you just hop,"
"Let's go and shop until we drop."

"Hang on," the eldest added swiftly,
"I'm feeling my age, now I'm fifty."
"Send the young'un window shopping"
"Or else I really will be dropping!"

So the young'un was sent on ahead
And on his tod, off he sped
To help the elder's ailing back;
The others stood around and yakked!

The young'un came back very late;
He apologised for making them wait
While he struggled with a pane of glass
The eldest poured tea from his flask.

"What on earth have you got there?"
He asked waving his hand in the air.
He put his hands on his head
As the young'un then eagerly said:

"I was told to go window shopping"
(The other shepherds' eyes were popping)
The elder said: "that's a figure of speech!"
The young'un dropped the glass on his feet.

"Yow-wee!" he yelled in despair;
(Thankfully he managed not to swear.)
He had to go on a hospital trip,
Though he said this was just a blip.

He gave the others his shopping list,
Which the elder waved in his fist.
The others went away and shopped;
They kept going until they dropped.

They arrived quite late to see the baby,
Joseph and the cherished lady.
They said: "What a precious boy,"
"He fills us all with Peace and Joy."

"We were as soon as we could be;"
"We had to stop in A & E."
He signalled the man with bandaged feet
"And then we found a blocked-up street."

They knelt, (though one was on his cloak)
"This tiny baby gives us Hope"
"And our hearts feel a huge lift."
They each presented a baby gift.

The first shepherd spoke on his bended knee:
"I honour the sportsman he will be."
"This is sure to be a hit"
"- his very first football kit."

Poor Joe couldn't believe his eyes;
Another gave a hoodie of medium size.
The thing was made of purple chiffon
With the words 'Keep calm and carry on.'

"Well, you can't get more British!"
Mary was a little skittish.
She sighed: "I suppose he'll grow into it!"
"I'll put it with the football kit"

Then Joe saw what the young'un had given
And his amazement was further driven;
It was a Macdonald's happy meal
And Joseph shook his head for real.

Seeing his face, another stepped in:
"Don't worry," he said with a grin,
"I have a better plan;"
"I bought you two weeks in a caravan."

"And Whitby's the greatest place on earth."
"I can do better" argued the third:
"This has a wonderful bit of charm;"
"I've sent you for a week to a farm."

"The Lake District has sights to behold
"And mountains to climb for the bold."
"Jesus can run on lawn in the space;"
"It really is a beautiful place."

Joseph put his head in his hands:
"Where do I start with the flaws in this plan?"
"Jesus has only just been born;"
"He's not old enough to run on lawn."

"And we might benefit from the fresh air,
"But how do I get the pram up there?"
The elder had been listening in:
"Don't worry," he said, "I brought gin."

"Jesus can have his very first drink"
"I apologise – the gin is pink!"
"I'm sorry if it makes your hair curl;"
"I thought you'd had a little girl."

"Gin?" stated Mary "Jesus won't be drinking!"
"Honestly! What were you thinking?"
Cried the blue-dressed cherished lady,
"Don't you know he's just a baby!"

The elder was unperturbed,
His suggestions would not be curbed.
Mary and Joseph were very sceptical
As he rummaged for another receptacle.

What happened next was such a relief
(Though they were aware it was probably brief)
He added, "Can I get up – it's hurting my knees"
And then produced his flask of tea.

"Maybe you'd like a nice hot drink,"
"Whilst I have another think."
"I see Jesus will be highly revered,"
All of a sudden the angels appeared.

They floated down and sang so beautifully;
"We have faced a lot of scrutiny"
"But the judges have reached a decision:"
"We've been picked for Eurovision!"

Meanwhile, knowing his gifts had flopped,
The elder popped to the corner shop.
After having another better thought,
He presented them with what he had bought:

Mary was astonished at what she received,
(He had a good one up his sleeve,)
He produced (as the angels' song got louder,)
A box of non-bio washing powder.

The Shepherd's Tale

Ally Schofield

The scene of Christmas

Inside the houses
adorned and full of cheer;
Rejoice! Rejoice! Christmas is here!

Roaring fire,
happy faces aglow;
Every home decorated
from head to toe;
A merry nutcracker,
a chimney of soot;
Owls outside give a hoot;

The wildlife of night is doing its bit,
While outside each house
is gaily lit;
For the marbled clouds
glancing down
And through the
night a glorious sound;
Joyful carols
sweep everywhere;
Amid the glistening frosty air.

Yes the people do love
Christmas time;
Bricks and mortar
dressed to the nines;
Oh the world likes to put on a show;
For a slowly melting man of snow.

Just As I Am

Beaming stained glass
in the church on the hill;
Where the people gather
to do thy will;
As the silver church bells
ring through the night;
We remember that awesome glorious sight

The angels gave such a merry chorus
Of great tidings that
they had brought us,
Of where once
a very brightly lit star,
Brought visitors from
both near and far,
It shone above the place
a babe sweetly slept
there a special promise was duly kept.

In church we answer to thy call,
And sing of the greatest story of all

We know the Prince of Glory has come;
Merry Christmas everyone!

The Scene of Christmas

Cherished lady of the blue

O cherished lady adorned in blue,
Such sweet sounds are made,
Embraced by hay and swaddling cloth,
And in the manger laid,
We yearly bless with seasonal love
that time of joyful cry,
That bleak, winter's night
a dawn of splendour, glorified.
For the angel brought word sweet and true,
O, cherished lady, of the blue.

Cherished Lady of the Blue

The greatest story in the world

I bring you news of a joyous story,
To tell you about the Prince of Glory.
The greatest story there has ever been,
It happened in a stable, poor and mean.
These words will tell of our salvation
And give great hope to all the nation.

Solemn stillness on a cold winter's night,
Angels singing and the shepherds' fright,
A borrowed stable, treasures given,
A special birth, a welcome addition.

'Twas clear up there in the starry sky
With wonder to amaze the eye;
One star brighter than the rest,
You see, I shone my very best.

Today I bring you great tidings glad,
But then there was not a room to be had.
For Mary and Joseph it was all in vain,
Too much to lose, and nothing gained.

A kind innkeeper, though, he tried;
A small offering he did provide.
A stable bare was all that they found
For the precious babe, born safe and sound.

Then angels' songs rang through the air,
Startled shepherds stopped and stared.
In awe and afraid they wanted to flee;
It silenced the lambs' loving bleats, you see.

'Fear not,' is what the angels sang,
'A gift from God is sent to man.'
'You'll find him in a lowly place,'
And off they went, now filled with grace.

Next my part in the story is here;
Great men I found and to them appeared.
For as a candle would light your way,
I, too, had my special part to play.

Wise men, camels, oh calm of night!
The guiding star to the infant light
Over hills and through valleys their path I lit.
They made quite a journey, I have to admit,
To see for themselves the special birth,
With gifts of gold, frankincense, myrrh

There asleep, with hay for his bed,
As the holy angels' songs had said,
As the wise men were told in their dreams,
Just one story – or so it seems.

Wise men, Joseph, donkey's trip,
Innkeeper, cattle, a hay-filled crib,
Shepherds frozen where they stood,
How I shone as brightly as I could.
Angel chorus, Mary mild,
Light of the World, this precious child,
In truth, this story has just begun
And He will bring hope for years to come.

I hope you have enjoyed my heartfelt words;
Now you have heard the greatest story in the world.

The greatest story in
the World

Prayer

A special place to gather my thoughts;
There my deepest worries are brought.
A safe haven to share hopes and fears,
To voice my joy or dry my tears
And from there; on I can plod
For this special place is prayer with God.

The constant

When it overwhelms you;
and you're on your own,
when you can't cope all alone;
When it towers above;
that tempest of fear,
The blizzard of loneliness no one can hear.

When anger as fierce as the wind's rage;
breaks out of its battered cage,
When your emotions; the biggest hurricane,
bring the storm of sadness all over again,
The answer is, it seems to me;
please God be always here with me.

For God is constant and He is there;
He is here and everywhere,
He is joy; He is care,
He is kind and He is fair
He is hope and He is pride;
He'll make you brave; push fear aside

When pain comes; He'll make you strong,
for not every sting you feel is wrong;
If there's no bad, there can't be good;
if it doesn't hurt when you know it should;
If you don't appreciate the way you feel;
the broken parts will never heal.

Embrace the bad when you feel small;
for God makes you feel invincible.

Precious memories

The section 'Precious Memories' and the poem 'To dream of the lost' is dedicated to all the beautiful souls we have lost – they are not really lost, they are watching over us.

'The setting sun' is dedicated to a very special lady – a great friend of the family, Carol Kenny. She is much loved and much missed, and I am very fortunate to have had inspiration from the beautiful, kind lady she was. It is a privilege to have known her and to be able to call her a friend. Thank you, Carol.

'Absolutely Grandad' is dedicated to my Grandad, the reverend Thomas Eric Simpson, whilst 'Grandad Peter' is dedicated to my other Grandad, Peter Schofield and 'The Northern Rock' to my Grandma, Sheila Schofield.

'The Blue Van' is dedicated to a very special friend, Jack Underwood, you are hugely missed.

'Our wise friend' is written for our late family friend, Ivy Blake, she too is very much missed and 'Norma' is written for Norma Price, also a good family friend. She is greatly missed.

To dream of the lost

When I dream it beckons to me:
"Come and visit," is its plea.
This place loves our company;
When you sleep let your mind drift,
For this place is God's gift.

It looks uninviting 'til you arrive;
It draws you in; you feel alive.
It radiates out its warmth;
Beauty at once will spring forth.
You know no bad can happen here
And they feel very near;
For here dwell absent heartstrings
And joy the sight of them will bring.

There, they're guardians of things misplaced
In Malposy, they are based.
That is how it is fondly known,
A place you're happy to the bone,
A land through which friendship flows
And also here are all those;

Odd socks,
Abandoned clocks,
Missing pens,
Long-lost friends.
Vanished legwarmers,
Awkward corners,
Forgotten thoughts,
Lessons not taught.
Rejected ideas,
Stifled fears,
Broken china cups,
Buses not turned up.
And anything one might mislay,
Carefully guarded and on display.

Occasionally with fortune one might meet
And with their owner again they greet;
We have the guardians to thank in this land,
For the job they do is really grand.

It's very special, don't you know?
For Malposy is where lost things go.

Absolutely Grandad

You could meet him once and never forget,
He was often involved in a garden project;
For outside and nature was his delight,
Said it lifted the spirits: well he was right.

He looked for the trees, not the wood,
And in everyone: tried to see good.
He saw the laugh in everyday life,
Which brought cheer in times of strife.

He was all about laughter and comfort,
And on hearing good news was most triumphant.
He never missed an opportunity to add some song;
Like "A policeman's lot is not a happy one".

Or "Just one cornetto, give it to me,"
Only one piece of broccoli, but always peas,
For lots of peas on his plate was what he liked,
"Everyone's a tutti-fruitti raisin"...but "don't tell him, Pike!"

If the queue stopped moving in front of us;
"Why are we waiting?" he would chorus.
Or with a fun and infectious grin,
If someone was slow he would sing;

"Will you go a little faster said the whiting to the snail,
there's a porpoise right behind us and he's stepping on my tail!"
With his dog collar on or one of his flat caps,
If someone themselves got in a flap;

"Don't panic, Mr Mainwaring!" he would shout,
Or sing, "I've got a little list" before going out.
And "What a wonderful thing is the pelican", he'd recite,
In his overalls or his cricket whites.
In his beret or sun hat, he would go by;
(He called it his straw benger: I don't know why).
He loved animals and the joy of fresh air,
And loved watching cricket from his armchair,

Or out there with them on the field;
Watching or playing with his eyes peeled.
And 'Chocolate pains'; a 'sheet of bread',
If you're hungry; go ahead.

And lettuce, by him known as 'rabbit meat',
He was always dressed pristine and neat.
He found beauty in every little birdsong,
And was always there if things went wrong.

"Sur le pont d'Avignon,"
Another one of his songs.
A different one for every occasion,
To burst into song he needed no persuasion.

"I go to Heligoland" another classic,
or 'Let's go to the fish quay' when stuck in traffic.
And when stood with the dishes all neatly stacked,
I spy, shiny silver in the vegetable rack;

It had disappeared before our eyes,
Now it's found again; the jolly vicar cries;
"Three cheers for the girl who found the lost fork!"
(Yes the cutlery decided to go for a walk).

Grandad Peter

I didn't get to kiss you goodbye
Before your time to enter the sky.
I didn't get to shake your hand,
Or to tell you that you were grand.

I wish I could see you,
To ask if you knew?
On your door I'd have knocked;
But your clock has stopped.

I delve and find my way through;
Something happy to remember you;
Good times on which to rely;
Memories my weeping eyes dry.

The northern rock

The lifeboat conforms to the tide,
Else she is battered from side to side;
She must go where the waters inform,
A choppy, chaotic, ferocious storm.

Somewhere off Whitby's coast,
In sea that earns respect from most,
Amid raging water stands a rock,
A test of time; nature's clock.

Withstanding all, never moving,
Wave beaten, but still refusing;
There steadfast in swirling deep,
Day and night, a watch to keep.

An atmosphere, cruel and spiteful,
The angry storm is just frightful,
But impenetrable stands the rock,
Taking on knock after knock.

The fury passes in a haze,
Nature's frenzy, a passing craze,
Her own defence she assists,
A demeanour infallible still persists.

Like a fortress or a stronghold,
Standing there, secure and bold,
She remains, undeterred,
She is my Grandma, unsubmerged.

The setting sun

It is sorrowful knowing the end has come,
But as beautiful as the setting sun;
One day this sun will rise once more
With the strength and kindness of before.
Although we know not exactly when;
Precious Carol, we will meet again.

Your memory is bathed in beautiful light,
As you go peacefully into night.
We will miss for sure our kindest friend
Who showed such courage to the end.
You always gave us your very best;
May angels sing you to your rest.

The blue van

A fount of good advice,
If help he could provide;
You never asked him twice,
On him you could rely.

Someone to turn to
When things were going wrong,
Even on a dull day,
He'd jolly you along.

There we'd all be playing
In our road, a little game;
The blue van would trundle in
"He's back!" we would exclaim.

The arrival took up its spot,
A staple of Lypiatt View;
Miss it – you could not,
That van of striking blue.

Out he'd pop with his black lab,
Through the open door,
Tired out from the day
And trotting on paws, four.

He was a man so kind,
A friend to one and all,
Thoughtful and hard to find,
One you could give a call.

I'll never forget the bold blue van,
And how he had our back .
He was to me, the best of man,
Our special friend, Jack.

Our Wise Friend

So many wise words
this lady had;
to share from what she'd learnt.
She did her best to prevent
getting our fingers burnt.

We'd go and visit when we could
Or with us she'd spend her time.
She'd never missed
Dad's Yorkshire puds;
Or his parsnip wine.

Norma

Norma herself
helped me out.
When I was stuck,
without a doubt:

Causing chaos in the loos,
the situation grew and grew,

(and the towel – that grew too!)

Norma came to my aid,
Solved the problem that I'd made
Lucky for me,
Norma was bolder;
she fixed the towel holder.

To think of others

To think of others

The section 'To think of others' is dedicated to each and every one of you who has – and still is inspiring me to write poetry, and all the lovely people who are reading my book.

'When a mouse roars' is dedicated to my Mam – yes, I'm aware that you don't like mice, but that is not why I wrote it for you. Thank you for always speaking up for me, even when no one would listen. You are a force to be reckoned with and don't ever forget it!

'Listen to the drowned' was inspired by a conversation with our good friend John Sibley, and also the scarecrow in 'The Wizard of Oz' who pointed out that some people with very little brain, have an awful lot to say!

'There is always something' is dedicated to my amazing gaggle of ladies in our EWG EWG (Eden Wild Goose Eating With the Girls) group, as Al has called it! (You have it in writing now Al!) Each trip hopefully acts as something, when times are difficult – a little chink of light to remind each of us that there is the support of friends to get you through. When any of you have trials in life – remember this poem. I might have started our little trips out, but I couldn't have done it without you all! Here's to many more trips! (Have your diaries ready girls!)

'Words of Hope' and many of the other poems in this section are written especially for anyone who is struggling. You are not alone.

I wrote 'To walk with friends' for our friend Debbie who comes to Holme Eden church and everyone who goes to the Cumbria Deaf association. Thank you for telling us about it Debbie, and for organising the walks, Boccia and coffee mornings.

Hope

A flower withers and dies;
A kite drops and will not fly.

A baby cries for he can't sleep;
A heart breaks, a person weeps.

The power goes and the eggs aren't done;
The sun is blocked when a cloud comes.

The kettle boiled but the tea's gone cold;
You've heard it before; that story's old.

A little obstacle seems insurmountable;
The problems pile and are not countable,

But take my hand I'll help you cope;
Remember there is always hope.

The real experts

I understand you have a degree,
But you don't have a degree in me;
Not in us, no;
Do you want to help us grow?
To really be in the know?

It might be about ticking boxes to you;
(Your intentions are good but that's the truth)
The important part gets missed out,
More times than I care to count.
The boxes need to be the right ones,
To have a positive affect upon,
Those who need these facilities,
To aid us in our disabilities.

Books say what they have been told;
But if I may be so bold;
How about asking the real experts?
(Come on – can it really hurt?)

Ask us what it is we need;
So that we can all succeed;
And just in case it's not occurred to you
We are all people too.

Lonely

How lonely must the moon feel?
When the stars are nowhere to be seen?
How lonely must the last puddle be?
Though it gives a lovely sheen.

How lonely does an email feel?
When someone forgets to press 'send'?
How lonely must a lost sheep be?
Parted from his friends.

How lonely must your school jumper feel?
When it's left behind on the bus?
How lonely is the grizzly bear?
Though he doesn't make a fuss.

How lonely does a deaf lip-reader feel?
When someone covers their lips?
How lonely must it be on the mountain?
On the highest peak, at the tip.

How lonely must the discarded pebble be?
Such a long way from its home?
How lonely is one egg;
Being boiled all alone?

How lonely must that one word feel?
In a 'yes' or 'no' text?
How lonely must empty buildings be?
Whatever happens next.

Just As I Am

How lonely are entertainers?
They're used to keeping people amused;
How lonely must the last carrot feel?
When all others have been used.

How lonely must one pheasant be?
Wandering the garden on his own;
Who knows what's goes through his head?
He seems ok, but he's still alone.

How lonely must people be?
If they are self-isolating on their own,
But I promise that I am thinking of you;
You are not alone.

Until the lady sings

Sometimes you think 'why me? – why?'
But all one can do in life is try;
Always do your very best,
And leave fate to do the rest.
Keep pushing yourself while you can,
And when it's needed – take a stand;
Everything can seem long and drawn,
But don't give up with holding on;
Life can be hard – all roundabouts and swings,
But nothing is over 'til the lady sings.

When a mouse roars

Don't judge a book by its cover;
What looks like fire can be cold.
A dull rock can sing, you will discover,
And all that glitters is not gold.

Not all jobs shout out glamour,
But all are as important as the next.
Each individual, be it person or animal;
Deserve to have the very best.

And if I have any advice to give you;
Remember not the peacock who loudly flaunts,
But often more worth listening to;
Is the tiny little mouse who roars.

When a mouse roars

When you see the sky cloud over

The dawn breaks through its sleep;
It's not a day you wish to keep.
The morning's full with rain and mist;
The daylight seems in such a twist.
It's still worth greeting the day;
Hidden treasures light the way.
Even though the sky is obscured;
With unpleasantness to be endured.

Though you feel down in the mouth
And things seem to be going south;
Somewhere light still shines through,
To tend to hope and make it new,
And don't believe what you've read;
You never know what's up ahead.
Don't start your day feeling blue;
There's always a different point of view.

Some hot tea in a chipped cup;
A spark of joy to lift you up.
Maybe some help from a friend,
To pick you up and help you mend.
The promise of tomorrow is not so far;
Though it seems a distant star.
Soon the slump will disappear;
You will hear what you need to hear.

So just hold on really tight,
Searching for that bit of light.
Keep looking for all you're worth;
To find your hope on the earth.
Just you look high and low;
When you find it you will know,
Somewhere is a four-leafed clover;
When you see the sky cloud over .

A grain of sand

Though you want it slow;
Time will surely race;
For it can never rest,
For long in just one place.

Time will pass you by;
Like the changing of the sky.
Yes, it will pass you by;
and time is truth not lies.

Time will pass you by;
Whether you smile or cry.
Time will pass you by;
A deep and distant sigh.

Time will pass you by;
It will happen anyway.
No matter how hard you try;
April still turns to May.

And no matter what you planned;
It will fall through your hands;
So make the most of what you can;
For time is like a grain of sand.

The small things

When an owl
Says twit to-woo;
It may be
a little thing to you;
Like opening a can;
crackle fizz pop,
To someone else
that sound means a lot;
You see the jug trickle
but to someone it pours;
Its a sound they've never
heard before.

A gushing stream;
the tweet of a bird
A meaningful thought;
or a kind word
A chirping cricket;
music of the mind
Hearing a voice;
for the very first time.

The special definition;
behind a known phrase
A blanket or a warm drink;
on a cold day
The lyrics of a hymn;
the blessing in a prayer;
or simply someone
just being there.

When you get lost;
being given a sign,
knowing that things
will turn out fine,
Sustenance for hunger;
water to quench thirst
Good news when
you've feared the worst;

Getting a bar of signal
when you're in a quandary,
Being the greatest friend
that you could ever be;
A hand to hold
when you're afraid,
A happy smile
on someone's face;

So remember the tiny things
they matter too;
And though it may seem
unimportant to you,
whatever you think
don't take them for granted;
for as certain as water
grows seeds that are planted;
and as sure as the sun
melts the frost;
to someone the small things
mean a lot.

Don't scream at me please

Outside is so unforgiving tonight;
It roars and rages with all its might,
The sky is angry without a doubt;
As though the storm is lashing out.

Among the noise the wind expels;
This is when I feel compelled,
It calls out to me the open space;
I roam beyond my safest place.

I venture into the big unknown;
Excited, nervous and yet alone,
I leave my familiar home behind;
With no idea what I might find.

Someone out here has cast a spell;
The noises I hear and know so well
Into an eerie silence do fade,
I am eager but still afraid.

Then for the calm after the storm;
And the dark hides well my true form,
But though I'm unseen in the background;
There are too many beings all around.

To shadow I keep; my fear is growing;
When gone is the dark that stops me showing,
There's danger when I lose my disguise;
For as always, the sun will rise.

I see water flowing out of stone;
I dodge monsters to cross the road,
The place is frantic and busy here;
But thirst takes over and buries fear.

I'm thirstily lapping up water there;
The beings around are everywhere,
There are no shadows to hide me here;
Mouths open wide; the danger is clear.

I long to be back in my home;
I'm so afraid for I'm alone,
However scared you may be;
Please please please, don't scream at me.

Be a lighthouse

There is a purpose you're on this earth;
And if you doubt how much you're worth;
If you feel lonely or full of regret,
If you've made a mistake just don't forget;
You are not one bee in a swarm,
You are the lighthouse in someone's storm.

Everyone needs a soothing ear,
There's always a reason for being here.
If their life becomes so frightening,
They might be shocked by sudden lightning.
You can offer them somewhere warm,
And give them shelter from the storm.

If they need refuge from stormy weather,
Or even wind as gentle as a feather.
Even if they tell you not to stay,
Be there in case they're blown away.
If life is kind or brings them pain,
Be around for the hurricane.

When on the horizon there is a shadow,
Something that brings another blow.
It can make you stand still and sigh,
But beware of a stormy sky.
For that is the a spirit of a storm,
It can be refreshing or full of scorn.

Whether they have a face like thunder,
Or whether they look and stare in wonder.
Whether they're totally thunderstruck,
Or it goes wrong and they're down on luck.
Whether they're dry under a brolly,
Or else as wet as a melted ice lolly.

Helping another will help you too,
Giving out smiles will get them through.
If someone needs help when the thunder rolls,
Go and slide down that fireman's pole.
Be there to help them take the strain,
For every storm runs out of rain.

There is always something

When you cry and count the cost;
And tell yourself that all is lost,
When you're ready to scream and shout;
I will arrive at the very last doubt,
The end of your tether; when you hit a brick wall;
The final bellow – the last port of call,
So don't despair; there is always me;
And all around you; a 'thing' I be,
But you need not ask for I will come;
My name is not 'no'; it is 'some'.

Nature feels

Always be proud of who you are;
for loving yourself
can light up the stars.

Let go of anger before it gets too deep;
for hate can make
the black clouds weep.

If you don't understand; ask the question once more;
For clarity can be like waves
reaching a far off shore.

When someone is hurting; be a rock for their pain;
for optimism is like sun rays
through the pouring rain.

Don't be jealous, be a well-wisher;
for envy can make
the upright trees shiver.

Share out your cheer to those feeling low;
For pessimism can cast
a long shadow.

Don't hide your wonder when you're met with delight;
For awe can make
the glowing sun bright.

Bask in natural beauty when you have the chance;
for nature's music
can make the trees dance.

Carry someone if you see them slip;
for loneliness can seem
like a mountain's highest tip.

Remember it's ok to be afraid;
For hiding fear
can make the moon fade.

Help others if you see them struggling in strife;
for happiness can bring
an ocean to life.

Always look for one face in a crowd;
for hope can reach
right up to the clouds.

Don't make your decisions far too soon;
for in confusion the stars
abandon their moon.

Don't keep wanting more than you have won;
for greed can eclipse
the land-hugging sun.

If someone's alone; be their prop;
For company can make you feel
on the world's top.

Look for humour once in a while;
for laughter can make
the silver moon smile.

Sad or happy don't hide your emotion;
For the tears of one person
can fill an ocean.

Homeless

As time moves on I'm left behind,
Out of sight and out of mind.
My old torn shirt worn day and night,
Is unkindly silhouetted by sunlight.
My tatty outlook friendliness deters,
I'm not worth knowing is what it infers

And my battered red boots,
The ones no one would choose.
They're no longer polished,
My dignity demolished.
They're clogged up with mud,
And move with a tired thud.

I sit by a shop doorway,
That same place everyday.
Or I lie on a park bench,
where I give off a stench,
Of unwanted and scorned,
Forsaken, forlorn.
Worth nothing - or so it feels,
What wouldn't I do for a bed and a meal.

A lorry passes by,
A hungry pigeon cries.
A women sweetly sings,
And a moment of joy it brings.
Or a postman's whistle,
A rose among thistles.
For in this life any sound,
Is worth to me a hundred pounds

Just As I Am

But still I sit feeling low,
For the welcome sounds come and go.
A crow overhead flaps his wings,
Then a phone starts to ring.
As a young man comes strolling by,
He stops and answers it with a sigh.
The man is presentable, nice and clean,
One of the people who is always seen.

He has everything he needs – more or less,
Polished shoes and well-dressed.
A black tail suit, a posh hat,
He stops at the bench where I am sat.
Back turned, he talks on the phone,
Then he leaves me there all alone.

Any kind word I had hoped to gain,
But just as water on a flame,
The help has already been relinquished,
And just like that my hope extinguished.
Before it is offered the hand snatched back,
And again it hits me like a smack,
When he and his briefcase walk away,
For this is my normal everyday.

Still I sit and worthless feel,
Still cold, unloved, without a meal.
If everyone passes without a glance,
Some of us here don't stand a chance.

Listen to the drowned

There are people who talk,
but all they do is sit and squawk
And they say nothing of use at all.

Other voices are never heard;
Though good thoughts
to them occurred.
They are the ones who need listening to;
Let us hear their point of view.

So in the crowds all around,
Please listen to those
Whose voices are drowned.

Snakes and ladders

On you plough; on you crack
One forward: two steps back
Don't lose heart; dry your tears
For every step to the rear
Another positive step is near

But is there more than treat or trick?
Is it more than carrot and stick?
Steps back don't have to be bad
Sometimes they can make you glad
Give a fresh view or make you stronger
Even if it takes a bit longer

Ying has Yang and Yang has ying
So any step is a win
Bad has good and good has bad
So stand tall and don't be sad

But sometimes it can seen a muddle
So please say if you struggle
What you feel really matters
And life can be like snakes and ladders

When you reach a ladder pointing high
There might be a snake nearby
But when you meet that lurking snake
Another ladder will compensate

And this might sound a little bit crackers
But remember you can slide down ladders
Or climb to triumph on the venom of a snake
Life's a bit of give and take.

To walk with friends

I walked a way with my friends
And even when the rain descends
We're in fresh air all along;
We make our way in such song.

For accompanying are many birds,
Making up their own sweet words;
A friend who knows, so we didn't get lost
Each happy step removed the cost.

A furry friend in good voice
At each fork made a choice;
Some gorgeous things our eyes did see,
Coveted in my memory.

And fresh air - it really matters;
All our worries nature scatters.
Each step, every twitter,
Every breath a piece of glitter.

So walk in nature with your friends,
And be grateful for every gem.

A lesson in patience

Is it irritating the hassle we cause?
Are we troublesome with our flaws?

Does our problem hinder you?
Would you rather have a brew?

All this bother is a pain in the neck,
So you'd rather take a rain check.

Your day seems opaque, not translucent;
You see us as just a nuisance.

Would it be better to be without?
If you have any doubt;
We live with our dealt cards
And the consequences that regards.
If our faults seem a grind
Inconvenience to you, you find...
If we make your boat capsize
No...we will not apologise.

I am here

Dear friend,
Heart of gold;
Keep your chin up, be consoled.
During dark days,
Things may seem,
A battle, a fight,
All upstream;
But just remember it will make you strong,
And I am here,
When it all goes wrong.
When your mind is full of doubt,
And through the dark,
There seems no way out;
Hold onto my words ,
When you lose your way,
And have faith that things will be ok.

When distant waves reach the shore

Unforgiving waters splash all around;
An angry threat to run me aground.
But when such thunder gives a roar;
I will not lie on the ocean floor.

I stay steadfast in a raging sea;
For I have strong resilience in me.
The tempest causes creaks and strains;
But upright here I will remain.

When the surf swirls round about;
With no hope of letting me out;
Furious tides make me a sieve;
But I have strength yet to give.

I still have much to strive for;
When distant waves reach the shore.
So in times of trouble, have fortitude;
Perseverance will see you through.

Be a positive force with
What you can give;
None conquer that perspective.

Before the last petal falls

Before the last petal falls: your time grows ever short;
For inner beauty cannot find a home, in the cruel sort.
Plod along with a heavy heart: you'll find nothing but despair;
Turn away from angry thoughts and show the world you care.

Before the last petal falls and time is running out;
You've seen how your anger hurts but still you're full of doubt.
It takes more energy to kick them while they're down;
Time to learn life's lesson - a smile surpasses a frown.

Before the last petal falls: the hour grows dark of late;
Anger always costs you – can you afford to pay?
Stay positive, and things look ever fine;
Look to a brighter future – leave the past behind.

Before the last petal falls or still the curse remains;
Look deeper inside you: the rose already fades.
The cruel that plagues you does more damage than you know;
The hole you've dug gets deeper: how many daggers can you throw?

Before the last petal falls: can you find the will?
Change your cruel heart – take a bitter pill?
Can you grasp the light and see the error of your ways?
Find it in your heart to love, enjoy some brighter days?

When the last petal falls: will you be kind in heart?
Show your inner beauty and make a brand new start.
Will the world open its arms to greet you: would you do the same?
Would you want to meet you: or turn away in shame?

Before the last petal falls

A frosty tale

It prods me with its fingers cruel,
Though it glistens like a jewel.
It's like having to crawl through
Thorns and they go for you.

Against the cold I duel and fight;
It seems to be full of spite.
I struggle to stay warm such a lot,
For frost and I, friends we are not.

Its bitter fingers, oh they cut!
I really hate the cold, but
What must the animals feel?
When it's so hard to get a meal?

Unyielding is frozen ground,
Though they search round and round.
Peck, peck; rattle rattle,
But they fight a losing battle.

The frustrated pheasant throws his bowl;
No one there – not a soul.
"Feed me, feed me," he shouts and crows,
"We're all hungry, and no one knows!"

For the hungry pheasant life is grim;
He lives up to the name we gave him,
He comes and taps on the patio door:
"Please sir, please, I want some more."

Regret

This enemy you can posses
Has an absorbing caress
It is a false friend
And it will break not mend

It sticks to you like glue
'Til it consumes you
It is constant, unending
And common sense bending

Regret can make you afraid.
This is not a nice comrade.
And it shuts doors
Don't let it shut yours.

Listen

The roaring polluted waters of disease,
Thoughtless and unkind,
Burst fiercely through the trees
With only destruction in mind.

It boasts relentless power to all who stand in the way;
Announcing more devastation,
Again and again tries to find those who sensibly hide away,
Enforcing isolation

The flowers of the NHS bridges build
Over the troubled brook so we don't stand alone.
As quick as humanely possible they utilise their skills;
Hour upon hour they work fingers to the bone.

While such tireless sorrow this river brings
The kind-hearted foliage in numbers grow;
These beautiful people are our wings
When the flow is fast and progress seems slow.

With a little bit of sweet comes a lot of bitter,
But there is a great beauty in this age;
When hope seems as small as the tiniest piece of glitter
Love and determination calm the river's rage.

The grateful clap for the flowers
And the prayers of the trees
Drown out the thundering power
Of the turbulent flow if only we
With the cheerful song of life persist.

And one more thing:

LISTEN.
No
REALLY listen.

listen

Words of hope

Remember, both sun and rain give you healthy grass,
Full or empty doesn't matter if you refill the glass.
In dark, there is light somewhere; be brave enough to look.
Be the person who gives, not the one who took.

Being afraid is OK; courage to continue counts.
Optimism is achieving; don't focus on doubts.
Why save the best till last? Do your best every time,
No hill is too big; no mountain too high to climb.

Set your sights high but be prepared to jump lower;
If you leave others behind, you need to go slower.
Find your voice when someone else is being ignored;
Ideas are possibilities, just waiting to be explored.

Hard is not impossible, if you decide to try;
Weakness is still strength, but dressed in disguise.
Mistakes are good lessons; everyone makes them, don't forget.
Instead of problems, see solutions, then you'll progress.

Embrace change and do all with love in mind,
Everyone needs someone; it costs nothing to be kind.
When you see mist, look for clarity and start to explore,
With every experience your understanding grows more.

Everything looks brighter when done with a smile,
Determination and drive will make it worthwhile.
Always try to be genuine, generous and honest,
Kept promises are golden to the one who was promised.

Just As I Am

If you see someone struggling, ask them why;
Improvement doesn't start with U, it starts with I.
Motivation is great; it gives you an easier task,
Admire the person who deserves it, not the one who asks.

Commitment to the game makes a truly great player;
If your heart is in it, your concentration won't waver.
Teach what you have learnt, and for what you have, rejoice,
Whatever has to be done, it is always your choice.

Hold your head high and be proud of your best,
Better to focus now, than to later have stress.
Fresh air and nature do wonders for the spirit,
A kind word is well spent and turns hours into minutes.

Winning is not important; the best lose as well,
Would you be your friend? Only you can tell.
Be a trampoline – absorb Energy; rebound more back,
If there's a bump in the road, take a breath and give it a crack.

Compassion has a bigger value than any kind of coin,
Silence has a voice sometimes louder than a noise.
If you open your heart then others will too,
Choose the best option when odds are against you.

Understanding is priceless; it makes a better song,
With love, and inspiration you can't really go wrong.
Conquer self-belief; you'll conquer the world without a doubt,
In every storm, remember,

Hope is the candle that never goes out.

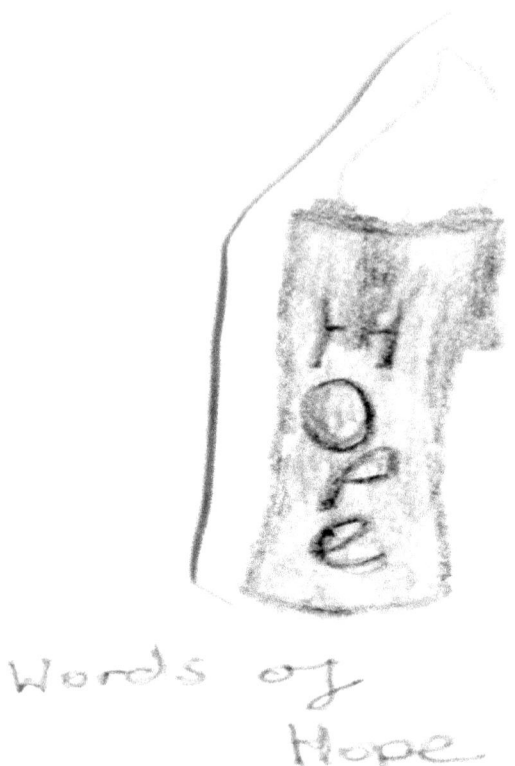

Words of Hope

www.ingramcontent.com/pod-product-compliance
Ingram Content Group UK Ltd.
Pitfield, Milton Keynes, MK11 3LW, UK
UKHW040648060525
5780UKWH00006B/14

9 781739 138196